"Deeply thoughtful! Beautifully written! I've watched Tricia teach, so I can't read this book without hearing her voice and seeing her passion add the ring of authenticity.

"Her heartfelt thoughts, expressed with hymn-like style, help me know God is wonderfully real and offer my hungry heart the ministry of certainty."

Doug Newton
Executive Director of Free Methodist Communications
Senior editor, *Light and Life* magazine

"Tozer once noted that the best preachers were not necessarily the most eloquent, but those who were 'awestruck in the presence of the God about whom they spoke.' Tricia Rhodes is a very eloquent writer, and yet her reverence and passion for Jesus found within these pages communicates on an even deeper level."

Matt Redman
Worship leader, songwriter

AT THE NAME OF
JESUS

MEDITATIONS ON
THE EXALTED CHRIST

TRICIA MCCARY RHODES

BETHANYHOUSE
Minneapolis, Minnesota

Published by Bethany House Publishers
A Ministry of Bethany Fellowship International
11400 Hampshire Avenue South
Bloomington, Minnesota 55438
www.bethanyhouse.com

Printed in the United States of America by
Bethany Press International, Bloomington, Minnesota 55438

Library of Congress Cataloging-in-Publication Data

Rhodes, Tricia McCary.
  At the name of Jesus : meditations on the exalted Christ / by Tricia McCary
Rhodes.
    p. cm.
  ISBN 0-7642-2636-3
  1. Jesus Christ—Name—Meditations. I. Title.

BT590.N2 R46   2003
232—dc21   2002152595

TRICIA McCARY RHODES is an author and speaker, a pastor's wife, and mother of two from San Diego, California. Her writings flow from twenty-five years of full-time ministry and a longing to glorify God by finding her greatest joy in Him.

———

If you are interested in knowing more about Tricia's ministry, you can reach her at:

New Hope Church
10330 Carmel Mountain Road
San Diego, CA 92129

(858) 538-0888, ext. 111

or e-mail at tpraynow@aol.com

To my son,
Jonathan (sent by God)
Samuel (asked of God),
whose life is a precious reminder to me
that God does all things well.

ACKNOWLEDGMENTS

Over the past several years my own sense of wonder and awe at the person of Jesus has grown beyond anything I ever could have imagined. I am deeply indebted to those who've continually extolled His supremacy, compelling me to let the glory of God in the face of Christ shine into the depths of my heart.

First, to my husband, Joe, who has faithfully preached the Word in season and out of season, how can I thank you other than to praise our Lord for His goodness in allowing me to be your wife? To have sat under your teaching for these twenty-seven years is a precious gift, one I never take for granted.

To David Bryant, whose message and life radiates the majesty of Jesus and the joy of knowing Him in a contagious way: Thank you for your ministry to me. I praise God for the way you've selflessly laid down your life for the kingdom. The body of Christ has truly been enriched.

To my prayer team: This could never have happened without your faithfulness. I found such hope in knowing you were always only an e-mail away, ready to intercede for the glory of our Lord. Thank you again and again.

And to Bethany House: Thank you for letting me write as God moves my heart. I pray continually that God would honor your desire to exalt Him. To Steve Laube, my editor and friend, somehow you always manage to bring out the best with kindness and grace. Thank you.

Above all, I say with joy inexpressible: Thank you, Jesus Christ my Lord, for saving me then, now, and forevermore. You are worthy. If you choose to use this book to shine your beauty into even one heart, I will have my reward. You are the delight of my life.

CONTENTS

This is a book about passion. About the resuscitation of passion. The kind of passion Paul's letters throbbed with, the kind that counts everything as loss just to know Jesus. This is a book about awakening godly fervor for Christ in light of all that He truly is. About igniting fresh encounters with the exalted Christ. On page after page, Tricia challenges us with the reality that Christ exalted and spiritual passion always go together.

Unfortunately, this kind of passion is a missing dimension in many modern Christians. Out of a stack of statistics documenting the church's condition, Dr. George Barna recently concluded: "Americans seem to have become almost inoculated to spiritual events. Overall, Christian ministry is stuck in a deep rut. Too many Christians and churches in America have traded spiritual passion for empty rituals, clever methods, and mindless practices. The challenge to today's church is not methodological. It is a challenge to resuscitate the spiritual passion and fervor of the nation's Christians" (taken from *The Second Coming of the Church*).

Barna uses the graphic word *resuscitate,* which the dictionary defines as "to set in motion; to stir; to revive from apparent death or from unconsciousness." It is a word about passion. And it is a word about this book.

Imagine, for example, mouth-to-mouth resuscitation. What do you envision? I see one person flat on his back and another responding with urgency. One face gets very close to the other; one mouth is set on top of the other; the air from one set of lungs flows rapidly and repeatedly into the other. Then there are groans, cries, and shouts of excitement as the victim sits straight up and laughs. Alive! Revived! Restored to a passion for life!

In a real sense, that's what Tricia Rhodes is looking for in *At the Name of Jesus*. Why? Because it's what she has first experienced in her own walk with Christ. This book is the effort of a woman of God to breathe new life into a reader's soul. But she wants far more than this. Her prayer (and mine) is that this book of meditations will provide our supreme Savior an opportunity to do for you what He did in John 20:22. Face-to-face with despondent disciples, paralyzed by fear, the resurrected Lord breathed on them (think *resuscitation*) and said, "Receive the Holy Spirit." That set in motion a passion and a mission that changed the world forever.

It can happen again. With you. With me. As the Spirit uses this book.

The first time I read Tricia's manuscript, I was on a transcontinental flight. And it was a good thing I had those five uninterrupted hours, because I simply couldn't put it down. You'll be blessed at the very outset by, of all things, the table of contents! Look at the thirty-one titles there that paint for us how exalted Christ is. Now consider this: Tricia gives us one attribute for each day of the month. Imagine how your life could be positively altered if you simply spent ten to fifteen minutes each day meditating on Christ's supremacy, using Tricia's compelling meditations, and then asking the Father throughout the rest of the day to breathe that specific reality of Christ into your heart and life. What a prospect that offers!

For an even greater impact, I suggest that you do what I did a few days after the flight: For each of the thirty-one days, read the meditation out loud. Tricia Rhodes is a uniquely gifted author; her books read well silently. But they make an even deeper impression when engaged audibly. My family and I have used her other writings in evening devotions, where I would read a short chapter to my wife, Robyne, and our three teens and watch how all of us were gripped by the power of Tricia's words and phrases. Her way of writing almost creates a sense of the presence of God! Try it.

At the very least, I urge you to read out loud the prayer that concludes each chapter. Make it your own. The prayers alone are worth the price of the book.

The hour has come for God to reawaken His people with nothing less than the supremacy of Christ. To reawaken us to hope and prayer and mission, centered on the Lord Jesus Christ for all that He is. To reawaken us to who our Redeemer is to us and for us, over us and within us, through us and ahead of us. In other words, to reintroduce us to Christ in the midst of us, the Hope of Glory (Colossians 1:27).

At the Name of Jesus is all about this. That's why it is genuinely prophetic. It challenges the ruts in our thinking about Christ. But it also summons us to match renewed minds with renewed passion. As Tricia Rhodes writes here:

> Surely Christ beckons us to repent of hearts that see Him so small we think our works enrich Him, our programs support Him, and our lives are indispensable to His plan. . . . To see Him move and work in power for His name's sake must become our consuming passion, deepening and intensifying as His Spirit takes control of our hearts. Let us settle for nothing less than the explosive inhabitation of the living Lord, that

our children, our neighbors, our co-workers, and, yes, the nations, may know at last that Immanuel has come.

Thousands across our nation are praying daily right now for this to happen. This book can help fuel our praying. The meditations can clarify more fully what we're actually praying toward. Namely, a Christ-initiated, Christ-glorifying resuscitation.

—David Bryant
President, Concerts of Prayer International
Chairman, America's National Prayer Committee

A *different Jesus . . .*

I set out to write a simple book, to put together a series of devotional passages on the names of Jesus. How lovely it would be: As Shepherd He guides me, as Physician He heals me, as Bread He feeds me, as Light He illumines me, as Redeemer He saves me, as Water He quenches my thirst, as Truth He enlightens me, as Life He energizes me. . . . All of these and so many more are precious realities upon which I could easily expound.

But there was a different Jesus. . . .

Somewhere along the way, the exalted Christ—the self-existent One in whom all the fullness of Deity dwells—hijacked my heart and set me on a course of discovery that has been both wonderful and disconcerting. The challenge to write of this Jesus seemed at first insurmountable, for in gentleness He'd revealed how I place myself at the center of even my loftiest thoughts of Him. To my dismay I realized that the Jesus I knew so well had been crafted not through the grid of *who He was* but of what He's done for me— how He feels about me, what He wants to give me, why I matter to Him, and so on.

But there was a different Jesus. . . .

The exalted Christ beckoned from afar, enticing me with His transcendent beauty until I knew that I must leave myself behind if I wanted to find Him in truth. Feeling at times like a dinghy thrust into a vast, unfamiliar sea, I tossed to and fro, crying out continually, *Who are you?* and *Why do you do the things you do?* My quest was nothing less than an encounter with the glorified Christ, the Eternal Other who dwells in unfathomable mystery.

Faithfully Jesus answered, expanding my vision of Him even as He rocked my heart, pierced my soul, and filled me in ever-fresh ways with His Spirit. I ache now with joy, and though it is bittersweet for the wasted years I knew Him not, still it is joy inexpressible and full of glory.

Perhaps He is calling you as well. Maybe you are hungry for a greater vision, a more magnificent understanding of this Jesus—the One whose glory is not enhanced or diminished by your presence on this earth but who delights to reveal its fullness to you. If so, I pray this book might serve as a tour guide, leading the way, pointing out the sights and sounds of a Jesus who's perhaps been in the shadows of faith for far too long. He is truly a different Jesus. May He indeed be worthily worshiped.

GOD

Yahweh, Elohim, El Shaddai, Adonai

REFLECT

Spend some time in quietness before God. Read Psalm 46:10 aloud, pondering both halves of the verse. Consider the greatness of a God whose exaltation cannot be thwarted, and let this knowledge still your heart as you seek to set aside the cares of this day.

For a moment try to mentally capture the image of the Jesus most familiar to you. What comes to mind first? What is He like? Are there any attributes of God you might find difficult to ascribe to Jesus? Why might this be?

Ask Jesus to come to you on this journey, to reveal himself in ways you've never seen before. Write a prayer of desire in your prayer journal.

READ

Choose one or more of the following passages to quietly ponder before reading the devotional below: John 10:30; Philippians 2:5–6; 2 Corinthians 4:3–4; Revelation 1:13–16; Revelation 19:11–12.

When I saw Him, I fell at His feet as a dead man.

REVELATION 1:17

Shut away on a tiny island in the Aegean Sea, the aging leader of the early church pondered his plight as a man banished from acceptable society. Winds carrying salty seawater provided the only relief from the afternoon sun as it bore down upon his well-worn face. Slowly John plodded along until he reached the refuge of a large rock, where he often knelt to pray. With charcoal from the night's fire, he made a mark to show another day had passed.

The rock's face was almost covered by now, but John no longer cared how much time had gone by—not since that one unforgettable day. Gazing into the distance, the wonder of it began to fill him once again. His weary eyes sprang to life as details of the incredible vision swirled around in his head like a hundred shooting stars all at once. . . .

It was a Lord's Day, the weekly highlight of his lonely exile, for always this day was spent in worship. Awakening early, he'd sensed an unusual stirring within. Quickly gathering ink quills and parchment, he set out, hoping that perhaps the Lord would grant him some fresh words for the fledgling churches whose welfare battered his heart continually.

Upon reaching his open-air sanctuary, the elder statesman of the Christian faith began to quietly praise his Redeemer. Soon tears flowed freely, his heart swelling with humble gratitude. Memories of walking with his Master along the shores of Galilee flooded his mind, filling him with the familiar yearning to touch that tender face once again. How he longed for just one more chance to lay his head against his Beloved's chest.

O my Lord, I thank you, for you came and gave me understanding so that I might know you, who are true. I praise you that I am in the truth, for I am in you, Son of God, Jesus the Christ. I worship you, true God and eternal life.[1]

Suddenly a frightening sound shattered the silence on the obscure island, shaking the ground beneath John's feet. It blasted forth in trumpet-like shrieks louder than the ocean's pounding roar, finally forming into words with a command to write. Flying to his feet, John turned to face the bellowing barrage.

At first all he could see were seven shining lampstands. But from their depths an alarming vision of a man beckoned him to draw near. John's whole being sunk down, his eyes gazing in spellbound wonder at the gleaming feet before him. All around them yards of glistening garments seemed to flow endlessly down. Trembling, John gradually raised his eyes, flinching at the beams of light that bounced off a golden breastplate. Wanting to run, yet unable to move, he could only stare, mouth agape, at the shimmering white wool-like clouds that enshrouded the head of the stunning specter.

With pounding heart, John leaned back, trying to take in the full force of this One whose presence seemed to permeate all thirty-five miles of the atmosphere on the island. What he saw next so astonished him that he knew he would never get over it. Eyes—piercing flames of fire—and a mouth wielding a two-edged sword comprised a face unlike anything he'd ever seen. So bright was the countenance that the full force of the sun seemed dim by comparison. In an instant John fell, face to the ground, like a man overcome in the throes of death.

What John saw that day was the glorified Christ—a sight so shocking he might never have rallied back to life had Jesus not knelt to tenderly assure him there was no need to fear. It is a vision we hear little of in the church today, perhaps understandably so. We are far more comfortable with the Jesus of Nazareth, who spoke kindly to adulterers and thieves, than one whose words slice the air with a sword of judgment. We feel more at ease with the Jesus whose eyes of compassion beckon weary souls to His side than the One whose flaming gaze pierces through our impurities. The face of Jesus marred by the blows of sinful man may grieve us, but in a warm way, for in His wounds we find the mercy that makes us new. It is not so simple to relate our notions of redeeming love to this face of Jesus that shines with such strength we cannot bear to look.

The incarnate Christ brought to planet Earth the face of *God*, and through His humanity we saw something never before revealed—the radiance of the Father's glory. The wonder and beauty of this is a source of comfort to every soul who has found in Him the joy of salvation. But if we are to worship Him worthily, we must always remember that the man Christ Jesus was *God* in the flesh—not some fanciful facsimile. He was and is fully *God*, the One who made the earth by His power, established the world by His wisdom, and stretched out the heavens by His understanding (Jeremiah 10:12).

When Jesus left this earth, ascending in a cloud, it was to return to heaven through the gates of glory, where myriad upon myriad of angels cried out in adoration as His Father placed the royal robes He'd left behind back upon His scourge-striped shoulders. Taking His throne, the exalted Christ resumed His reign as the one true *God*, all things at last subject to Him.

This is the Jesus who appeared to John that day on the isle of Patmos. There, in majestic splendor, He reminded the awestruck exile of the truth that transforms everything. *Do not be afraid; I am the first and the last, and the living One; and I was dead, and behold,*

I am alive forevermore, and I have the keys of death and of Hades (Revelation 1:17–18).

This is the ultimate reality, the unspeakable wonder reserved for those who believe—that though He came to earth and died, Jesus is and has always been the living *God,* and He alone holds the keys of life and death. Let the church rejoice, for our Lord reigns! He who once walked among us now fills all things with His terrifying and triumphant beauty. Let us fall down in worship at His glorious feet (Revelation 1:18).

RESPOND

What has been your experience of the majesty of Jesus? Is there mystery in your meditation? Wonder in your worship? Are there moments when His transcendent beauty so consumes you that you long to offer your life completely, bowing before Him with reverence and awe? Prayerfully consider this:

Jesus is God, the Creator and Sustainer of all things, who at this very moment holds the entire fate of the universe and every creature on it in His hands. Consider the sheer weight of Jesus' power, His glory and marvelous essence. Ask Him to reveal himself afresh to your heart. Wait upon Him, worship Him, and write a prayer of response.

A Prayer

Jesus, precious Jesus, who spilled your blood for me, how can I grasp that you are also the God of transcendent power? In my struggle to reconcile the two, I confess that at times I've espoused a sort of domesticated version of your deity. It seems so natural to embrace you as sweet, warm, tender, good, accepting, comfortable. Yes, you are these, but oh, so much more. You are worthy of greater honor—you who hold the worlds together by your power and will one day crash through the cosmos with the fire of judgment in your eyes. Let these truths tenderize and terrify my heart that I might offer worship proportionate to your worth. Open my eyes to the fullness of your being until I grasp the weight of the reality that you, Jesus, are fully and completely God.

JESUS

Jehoshua, Yahweh, Yahweh Is Salvation, Savior

REFLECT

Quietly wait before God, asking Him to manifest His presence to your heart today. Breathe deeply, seeking to release the distractions and cares of the day as you focus on Him. Offer Him your whole self, your undivided attention for this time. Ask Him to give you abundant grace (divine enabling) to learn of Him today.

Consider the following questions: What is God's deepest motivation for all He does? Why did He send Jesus? Why has Jesus forgiven your sins? John writes very tenderly to us as children that our sins have been forgiven "for His name's sake" (1 John 2:12). What do you think this means? Read Psalm 79 as a prayer to the Lord, asking Him to reveal the truth behind His purposes and to burn in your heart afresh a love for the name of Jesus during your time today.

READ

Slowly ponder one or more of the following verses before reading the devotional that follows: Matthew 1:21; Acts 5:40; Acts 21:13; Colossians 3:17; John 20:31; 2 Thessalonians 1:11–12.

> *So they went on their way from the presence of the Council, rejoicing that they had been considered worthy to suffer shame for His name.*
>
> ACTS 5:41

Around the year A.D. 200, the gruesome death of a twenty-two-year-old woman named Perpetua became fodder for the frolicking crowds in a coliseum in northern Africa, a province of Rome at the time. Her crime was one of loving Christ, of having found in Him the joy of salvation and, as a result, refusing to offer sacrifices to the Roman gods. It was an offense punishable by death.

Her execution came at the end of a long confinement in a dark dungeon, where the Roman authorities had tried to get her to recant through continual browbeating. At times they dragged her to the marketplace for interrogation, glorying in her public humiliation. Once as she stood before the large crowd in disgrace, her aging father arrived carrying her infant son. Pressing his way up the platform, he pleaded with her to offer a sacrifice for the sake of her baby. When she refused, the authorities knocked him off the platform, adding grief upon grief.

On the dismal day of her death, the brave young woman was shoved into the arena, where the stands erupted in gleeful cries as a bull darted toward her in mad fury. When it succeeded in goring her side, Perpetua flew into the air, landing several feet away in a bloodied heap. Quickly she pulled herself up, seeking to comfort the other martyrs in the arena. Reaching out to embrace her dear friend Felicitas, she called to the young men, "You must all stand fast in the faith and love one another, and do not be weakened by what we have gone through!" The authorities then sent in a terrified gladiator who was able to land the fatal blow only after

Perpetua assisted him in holding the sword to her throat.

Stories of believers who willingly lay down their lives for the cause of Christ confound me. A bulletin board in my kitchen holds an ever-increasing collage of articles—short, sobering obituaries gleaned from obscure sections of the newspaper—that may be the only kind of memorial many modern-day martyrs will have. In the gospel-light milieu of my generation, saints such as these are an anomaly, and I find myself examining their lives, pondering what energizes them to press ahead with such zeal.

The answer is perhaps reflected in something Luke wrote about the apostles after their first taste of persecution. Imprisoned, flogged, and warned not to speak in the name of *Jesus* again, they went on their way, Luke says, *rejoicing that they had been considered worthy to suffer shame for His name* (Acts 5:41).

For a Jew, a person's name—whether given at birth or taken later in life—was purposeful, reflecting the very essence of who they were, a sacred trust that they were born to fulfill. One's name was the same as their reputation—thus they did everything to live up to it. The name *Jesus* in Hebrew was "Yehoshua," translated *Yahweh is salvation*. When the angel announced this name to the teenage Mary, it carried with it the weight of divine promise, the fulfillment of a joyful destiny for everyone who would believe.

For the disciples, the name *Jesus* was replete with holy significance, a perpetual reminder that not only had they been saved from sin and death but also one day they would enter eternity to dwell in His marvelous presence. No one could have known the yearning such a thought wrought within their hearts.

These were the men who had left everything to follow *Jesus.* For three years they'd seen the beauty of His love, the radiance of God himself shining in all that He did, the touch of miracle upon life after broken life. They were eyewitnesses to His majesty and watched firsthand as He paid the price to bring salvation to their sin-sick souls. Devastated by despair upon His death and then dumbfounded at His resurrection, they had marveled together as the last vestiges of His humanity disappeared into heaven before their eyes.

When Christ's Spirit descended upon them at Pentecost, these same men were utterly changed. A compulsion to speak of His name drove them to the streets, where they could not stop talking of the wonder of His glory. The reality of their salvation so radically altered their worldview that they saw suffering as a privilege, for it gave them a chance to demonstrate their zeal for the worth of *Jesus,* their Savior.

The name of *Jesus* is a precious jewel, a treasure that ought to fill every redeemed soul with wonder and overwhelming delight. If it doesn't, perhaps we've not yet understood the miracle of salvation, the absolute marvel that we who once scorned our Creator to go our own arrogant way are now welcomed into His embrace, indeed even inhabited by His holiness. The name of *Jesus* ever reminds us of the blessed truth that *Yahweh is salvation*—that what we could never do, He has done, fulfilling the sacred trust inherent in His name. Those who saw Perpetua and her fellow martyrs die called it a day of triumph, observing with awe that the group proceeded from the prison to the amphitheater as if they were on the way to heaven.

> They had gracious and happy countenances. If they trembled, it was not with fear but with joy. Perpetua followed the group with light steps, as a true bride of Christ. She, the beloved of God, moved all who saw her with that great spirit in her eyes.[1]

Jesus—*Yahweh is salvation*—and oh, what a glorious salvation. This name before which every knee—in heaven and earth and under the earth—will one day bow has the power to astound and fortify and energize all who sing the song of the soul set free. *You shall call His name Jesus, for it is He who will save His people from their sins.... Therefore also God highly exalted Him, and bestowed on Him the name which is above every name* (Matthew 1:21; Philippians 2:9–10). Beautiful name, precious name, blessed name ... Jesus.

RESPOND

Knowing Jesus is a treasure so extraordinary that His followers for more than two thousand years have joyfully embraced suffering and even death for His name. Ponder this for a few minutes. What have you seen of this Savior through the eyes of your heart? Is your zeal for Him driven by the wonder of what you've seen? Does your experience of Him cause you to love His worth, to yearn to see more, to live to make it known in your words and deeds? Does joy in who He is drive you forward in your walk of faith?

Offer a prayer of desire, an honest cry to Jesus to reveal himself and the wonder of salvation in His name. Acknowledge that you are helpless to conjure up such an experience ... determine only to press into knowing Him, trusting in His grace to open your eyes and heart. Whatever you have known of Him, He delights in a heart that longs for more. Write a few sentences expressing your desire today. Spend a few minutes in silence, waiting for Him to reveal himself to your heart. Worship Him.

A Prayer

Jesus, name above all names, I am lost in the wonder of my salvation. My heart beats faster and my spirit soars at the very mention of your name. Yet my love for you is bittersweet, for I live in a world that spurns you. I grieve when believers take your name lightly, and I am broken when lost souls ignore you alto-gether, oblivious to your infinite worth. I live for the day when every eye will look upon you and know the truth at last. Until then, consume my soul with life in your name. Let me pray to see it hallowed, suffer to see it exalted, and live to see it worthily worshiped—Jesus, wonderful Jesus.

SPIRIT-GIVER

Baptizer, Benefactor, Saturator, Infuser, Replenisher

REFLECT

Take some time to quiet your heart today. As you breathe deeply, rest in the assurance that you don't have to accomplish anything, that God simply wants you to drink from himself. Thank Him that His Holy Spirit has come to dwell within you.

What has been your experience of the Holy Spirit? Is He personal, real, a pulsing presence day in and day out? This is Jesus' desire for you. Stop right now and open yourself to whatever He wants to give you today. Ask Him to pour His Spirit without measure into your heart that His name might be exalted by your life.

READ

Read as many of the following passages as you can, asking God to give you fresh awareness of their meaning. Then read the devotional. John 1:33–34; John 7:37–39; John 3:34–35; Matthew 3:11; John 16:13–14.

> *For He whom God has sent speaks the words of*
> *God; for He gives the Spirit without measure.*
>
> JOHN 3:34

I am a seasoned veteran of Sunday school, a charter member of the church nursery. After half a century I can still be found within the walls of a sanctuary most Sunday mornings. As a child I went to church to learn God's Word, and one thing I knew for sure was that we were a people of the Word.

Year after year our teachers instructed us in the fine points of faith while we yawned in eager acquiescence. Everything fit together, and that was nice because we didn't have to be afraid of religious renegades infiltrating and defiling Christ's church. We could spot them a mile away.

As a college student trying to understand Scripture on my own for the first time, I found my equilibrium often upset. The Bible seemed more, in Annie Dillard's words, "like a scandalous document" than the concise compilation on God I'd gotten growing up. Dillard relates how she thought if her teachers had really read the thing, they would have hid it for its dangerous implications. Instead she notes, "Our teachers bade us study great chunks of it, and think about those chunks, and commit them to memory, and ignore them."[1]

I remember reading John's words about Jesus coming to baptize us with the Spirit and with fire, and I was sure that my concept of the Holy Spirit had been sorely deficient. I'd always been taught that we get the Holy Spirit when we pray the sinner's prayer, and that is that. We get IT ALL. Period. No subsequent outpourings, no ecstatic experiences, nothing but the Spirit of God come to live within our hearts like a guest who shows up for dinner and decides to stay for good. Though news of His coming brought gladness to our souls, it seemed for all practical purposes as if He'd gone into retirement upon arrival.[2]

In looking to see how those outside my tradition handled the outlandish implications of John's words about Jesus, I was disappointed that they had their own box into which the Holy Spirit nicely fit. Some boxes were bigger or of a more peculiar shape, but boxes they were. We had it wired; we'd all in some fashion made the Spirit a manageable component of our Christian walk.

But those words—*baptize* and *fire*—troubled me. As a good Baptist, I knew that baptism meant going under all the way, being drenched, dunked, every inch submerged. That, plus a mental picture of forest fires burning out of control, made me wonder how anyone thought we could ever get IT ALL at any point in time— whether in salvation or in some second, third, or even fourth blessing.

Scripture refers to the Holy Spirit as a river, a turbulent force that surges along, destroying debris in its wake, sweeping up anything caught in its path. The prophet Ezekiel, in his fantastic vision, sees himself going in ankle deep at first, then up to his knees, and finally swimming in water impossible to ford at all (Ezekiel 47).

Reading that made me think that immersion into the Spirit of God must take a lifetime, that there would be tumultuous times when I'd have to hang on for all I was worth. Like Shel Silverstein's poem about the boa constrictor, I am in the process of being swallowed by a force infinitely greater than my mind can conceive. "Oh gee, he's up to my knee . . . oh my, he's up to my thigh . . . oh fiddle, he's reached my middle," and on it goes.

Given the all-consuming nature of the Holy Spirit, it seems inane to have ever thought He would do His work in one take. Perhaps that's why when Paul commanded us to *be filled* with the Spirit, He used a verb tense that indicates process—more literally translated *keep being filled* (Ephesians 5:18). The Holy Spirit is as boundless as the Godhead of which He is a part, and I rejoice, therefore, that in my lifetime I will never get IT ALL.

Meanwhile, a day is coming when Christ will manifest His reign at the right hand of the Father, when every enemy will be silenced and every believer will bow in joyous submission, casting their crowns at His feet. Until then, He is about establishing His kingdom in the hearts of men. To that end He promises to give the Spirit *without measure* (Luke 11:9–13; John 3:34–35).

The Holy Spirit's one agenda is to glorify Jesus, to make known in and through and to us the reality of the exalted Christ and to empower us to joyfully yield control of our lives. It won't happen all at once, and thus Jesus invites us to keep coming back, to keep drinking at the well of His glory, promising that as we do, gurgling springs of God-Spirit will well up within, transforming us from the inside out.

The river of God runs as wide as His mercy, as deep as His love, and as ponderous as His passion for His own glory. Jesus, *Spirit-Giver*, will come to us as raging fire and rushing water—breathing, baptizing, infusing, replenishing, and saturating our souls until that day we enter eternity and know at once that we've only just begun to get IT ALL.

RESPOND

When you think of Jesus as the Spirit-Giver, how does your view of the Holy Spirit change? What kind of box have you placed Him in? Some people box Him in as something you simply claim by faith, as if experience is irrelevant. Some people do the opposite, boxing Him into ecstatic experiences or dramatic signs. What does your box look like? As you hear Jesus speaking over you His desire to fully immerse, to drench you with His Spirit and with fire, what do you think He is saying? Whether you feel you've experienced this or not, take the time today to ask Him to take you deeper into the river. Ask Jesus to fulfill this promise and wait upon Him with an open heart.

The primary work of the Spirit within us is sanctification—a lifelong process of setting us apart to belong wholly to Christ. The most powerful manifestation of God's Spirit is a life completely committed to exalting Christ through obedience. As you consider your experience of the Holy Spirit, how is He manifesting himself? In what ways do you see your life exalting Christ through increasing obedience to His Word?

We will never grasp the depths of the Holy Spirit, for He is the infinite I Am, the breath of very God come to live within us. He is a gift from Jesus to those who belong to Him, and He promises to be ever welling up from the depths of our being, filling us with joy and transforming us by His power. Ponder this for a few minutes. Write a prayer of response.

A Prayer

Jesus, how you must smile at my foolish notions. To think I could ever explain or contain your Spirit—that infinite, bound-less, swirling breath of life you blew into my soul so many years ago. Oh, how graciously you've led me into the river that flows from your throne and out of my innermost being. I long for the day, my Spirit-Giver, when I am in so deep that I do nothing but yield to the current of your love, letting you wash over and in and through, transforming me for your glory. For this I yearn, for this I will come again and again, O blessed Spirit-Giver.

CREATOR

Architect, Designer, Originator, Mastermind, Engineer

REFLECT

Spend a few minutes in quiet prayer, then read Psalm 119:1–4, personalizing it as praise back to God. Looking back over the last few days, what have you seen of the glory of God in creation? Do you find yourself taking the time to listen to the language of His works? When you notice a sunset or feel a warm breeze, do you stop and think of the Creator, whose wonders are being displayed?

What do you think it means that you have been created through Christ and for Christ? Ponder this for a few minutes, asking the Holy Spirit to reveal truth in your time with Him today.

READ

Read the following verses and then the devotional: Colossians 1:16; Revelation 4:11; 1 Corinthians 8:6; Job 38:6–7.

All things came into being by Him.

JOHN 1:3

In a physics lab thirty miles west of Chicago, thousands of the finest minds in science converge daily around a massively complex machine. Their agenda? To discover an elusive elementary particle that they say will tell us why the universe is made of something instead of nothing . Scientists theorize that this particle with a name but not yet a face is that which gives "buffalo, geese, prairie grass, and all the other things in the universe a chance to be."[1] The quest to find it has become the greatest goal in physics.

To those who delight in and to those who are baffled by the complexities of quantum physics, the Mind behind the mysteries of mass and matter offers the same amazing possibility—a personal encounter with Him. Scripture tells us His name is Jesus, the One through whom all things were made.

In a moment transcending time, as Father, Son, and Spirit communed in love and joy, a plan was put into place to create a world through which God's glory would shine. It was a plan of wonder and grace that He who had need of nothing resolved to multiply the manifestation of His beauty for His own pleasure and the enjoyment of men He would make in His image. The Genesis account leaves much mystery as to how it all happened, but we know the Father spoke, the Spirit moved, and through the Son, creation occurred.

Imagine the magnificence of those moments. Were the morning stars singing glorious arias as the *Creator* brought into being a bug-eyed mudskipper that would spend its life building elaborate mud castles as mating dens? Were the angels shouting for joy as He created termite queens that could lay more than one thousand eggs a day, or army ants who'd march by night in columns half a million strong?

Did belly-shaking laughter bubble up within the Godhead as Jesus blew grains of pollen wafting through the air in thousands of unique shapes we have yet to see with the naked eye? Did the

Father and Spirit dance with delight upon the two hundred thousand square miles of tabletop mountains Jesus sliced into existence in Venezuela, while sowing their soil with more than ten thousand species of plants we have yet to discover?

I remember a young college student's response to the question of why God created the world. "For the fun of it," he called out, and though his answer was unsettling in its flippancy, it revealed a profound truth. As Paul wrote to the church in Colossae, *All things have been created by Him and* for *Him* (Colossians 1:16, emphasis added). The *Creator*'s own joy is the reason for which all things came to be. Through Jesus the glory of the Godhead emanated this montage of ecstasies we call creation, wonders that delighted His soul and now ours.

But far more wondrous than the sparks that flew from His fiery essence is the Flame itself, the Consuming Fire, who makes us His own. The kaleidoscope of His creation rings with a clarion call to muse on this Maker, to fall down in absolute awe and worship. For the greatest marvel is yet to come—not in the creatures or the cosmos but in the *Creator* who brought them into being and upon whom we will one day have eternity to gaze in rapture.

RESPOND

God created the world to display His glory—not out of any need or deficiency but as an overflow of delight in His own being. What might be some faulty beliefs you or others have had concerning why God created the world?

Jesus is the cause behind all creation, the Architect of every living thing. Yet the most magnificent wonders of creation will never compare to the incredible gift of seeing the Creator face-to-face. Since creation displays His glory, in what ways might various aspects of it give you a deeper grasp of Him? Ponder this and write a prayer of response.

A Prayer

O Jesus, Creator of the cosmos and of my soul in which you have come to dwell, how can I ever comprehend you? I look at the world with its wonders and works and whispers of glory, and I am dumbstruck. When I consider that you gave me all this to enjoy—sun and stars, oceans and rivers, hummingbirds and hyenas, wheat grass and whippoorwills, canyons and caverns, bumblebees and buttercups—I can only be in awe and like David reply, "What is man that you take thought of him?" Can we even fathom the tiniest taste of your beauty? Will we ever on this earth grasp a glimpse of the grandeur that flows from your throne? Even here in this temple of creation with its mark of sin, I behold your touch and can only cry, "Holy." And so I bow, for what else can I do?

REDEEMER

Recoverer, Restorer, Purchaser, Buyer, Procurer

REFLECT

Come before the Lord today in stillness and rest. Breathe deeply, seeking to settle into the sense of His glorious presence. Let the word *Redeemer* move in your mind, meditating on its beauty. Jot down a few thoughts of what this means to you.

Today you may be looking at a facet of this name you've not seen before. In fact, it may seem unusual or strange compared to the way you are used to thinking about your redemption. Ask God to give you an open heart, to illumine your soul to the spiritual realities He wants you to see today. Remember that we are completely dependent upon the Holy Spirit for the truth of God's Word to change us.

READ

Read a few of the following verses and then the devotional: Job 19:25–27; Isaiah 44:24; Titus 2:14; 2 Samuel 7:23; 1 Corinthians 6:20. Take time to let the words resonate within. Do not rush.

As for me, I know that my Redeemer lives . . .
whom my eyes will see and not another. My heart
faints within me.

JOB 19:25, 27

In his wonderful three-volume anthology entitled *The Unfolding Drama of Redemption,* Graham Scroggie beautifully unveils Scripture as a spiritual organism with every part connected to the larger whole. From the creation to the consummation of the age, he carefully communicates how the multi-hued threads of God's Word are woven together into an eternal tapestry. And from the beginning it is clear that the essence of all Scripture distills in the being of Christ, our *Redeemer.* He is the hero, the lead character, the one who gives significance to all other players and meaning to every dramatic scene. Scroggie writes:

> In the Old Testament Christ is predicted; in the Gospels
> He is present; in the Acts He is proclaimed; in the Epistles He
> is possessed; and in the Revelation He is predominant. . . . In
> this view all parts of the Bible, from books to verses, consti-
> tute a divine progressive revelation of redeeming love; God
> and man meet in the One who is the God-Man.[1]

Indeed, the revelation of redeeming love is a beautiful theme that resounds in songs and sonnets from God's Word and the very fabric of our lives—not only in human history but in our personal stories as well. We are lost souls, ever prone to sin and the self-destruction that accompanies it. We are born with a yearning to be set free and a longing for someone grand enough to sweep us out of the bondage of our brokenness. The unfolding drama of redemption is the *what* of God's Word, the description of our condition and its cause, of a solution and its source.

But there is something that gives breadth and depth to the *what* of redemption, and that is the *why*. Why did God redeem us? To fail to lay hold of this is to run the risk of placing man at the center of redemption's story, causing us to approach Scripture like a year-book, always hoping to find our own picture on its pages and disappointed when we don't.[2]

But as Scroggie so brilliantly sets forth, Christ—not humanity—is the centerpiece. From the beginning of His Word until the end, God makes it clear that as much as He loves us, He is motivated not first and foremost by us but by himself. *But I acted for the sake of My name. . . . I, even I, am the one who wipes out your transgressions for My own sake* (Ezekiel 20:9; Isaiah 43:25). This is a difficult thought—it seems to fly in the face of the plethora of teaching about our worth, our value, our specialness to the heart of God. How can it be that God forgives and redeems us for His own sake?

To begin to grasp this, we must look at the very nature of sin. When God created Adam and Eve, He offered them the most exquisite mystery His majesty might afford, the privilege of dwelling in His presence, enjoying intimate communion with Him. Adam and Eve ate the forbidden fruit because they believed a lie that there must be something more, something better; indeed, that the presence and person of God was not enough to satisfy their souls. This one sin polluted all of creation with a tragic and insidious world-view repudiating God's sovereign sufficiency.

Since then, we have continually sinned by trading the infinite worth of God for vain worldly substitutes, saying in essence that there is a greater gain, a more powerful purpose for living than the Creator who gives us breath. For God to allow this to go unpunished would imply careless indifference, a casual sharing of His glory that in the end would deny His very divinity. If He is God, there simply can be nothing better. By His very nature, God must extol and uphold His own honor and worth, destroying anything that sets itself above Him. *For My own sake, for My own sake, I will act; for how can My name be profaned? And My glory I will not give to another* (Isaiah 48:11).

God could have acted for the sake of His name by simply dooming all of us to eternity in hell. This is the miracle of His mercy—that through Jesus Christ, our *Redeemer*, God upholds His own worth by making a way for us to know Him. Being cleansed, forgiven, and set free from the impotent treadmill of banal glories, we can at last taste and see and know His supreme glory. As He manifests himself in and to and through us, our hearts will burn with desire to magnify Him, to make Him known . . . until every tribe and tongue has heard, until the whole earth is filled with His glory. This is God's plan. This is what it means for Him to redeem us for His own sake.

The unfolding drama of redemption reveals hidden wonders that even angels long to understand and at which we will spend all of eternity marveling. Because God alone comprehends the full worth of His being, we can only be awestruck when we see to what lengths He goes to preserve His name. To know that our *Redeemer* lives, that we will one day stand before the One who laid down His life that we might gain His glory, can only stir within us hearts that ever live to glorify His name every day on this earth. *O for a thousand tongues to sing our great Redeemer's praise.*

RESPOND

Jesus our Redeemer has paid the ransom with His own blood not only to deliver us from slavery to sin but also to enable us to satisfy our souls in Him. In what ways might we tend to view our salvation as ultimately about us instead of God? How would understanding the *why* of redemption change the way you approach prayer, God's Word, fellowship, and service?

God did not pay such a costly price to redeem humanity primarily because of their need but because He wanted a people through whom He could make a name for himself, a people who would both gain His glory and give Him glory through joy-filled obedience. In what ways are you experiencing the glory of God? In what ways does the flowing out of your life glorify Him? What kind of a name for himself might He gain by the life you live?

The joy of joys that we have been purchased for is for the moment we will see God, when our Redeemer takes His stand on the earth. Such a wonder must continually stir and motivate us to greater obedience. Ponder this and write a prayer of response.

A Prayer

Blessed Redeemer, precious Redeemer, it seems now I see you on Calvary's tree. That image resonates in my heart and still I feel the thrill of it, O God, for my ransom has been paid in holy blood. Lord, why do I struggle so to grasp that you didn't redeem me primarily for my sake but for yours? And humbly, Lord, I must ask if your plan is really working. I look at my own life and at your church, and more often it seems we bring shame to your name than glory. We act more like masters of our fate than a people for your own possession. O God, remind me moment by moment that you redeemed me for yourself, that the costly blood you spilled has no value outside of a life that glorifies your name. Prepare me for that day you will take your stand and I will behold at last your face, my precious Redeemer. Even the thought makes my heart faint with joy.

SON OF MAN

Incarnate One, Come in the Flesh, Born of Earth

REFLECT

What does it mean that Jesus became man? Consider that His greatness, His power, His eternal nature, and the worship due Him as a result were laid aside when He came to earth. As you come to wait upon Him today, ponder the mystery that God became a man, taking on weakness and struggle, even temptation to sin. Have you grown so accustomed to this thought that it holds little mystery to you? Does it still have the power to fill you with awe?

Be still in God's presence and ask Him to give you insight into the depths and beauty of the reality that He came and dwelt among us.

READ

Read the Scriptures provided and the devotional that follows: Matthew 8:20; Philippians 2:5–7; 2 Corinthians 8:9; Isaiah 53:2–3.

And He began to teach them that the Son of Man must suffer many things.

MARK 8:31

What if God was one of us?
Just a slob like one of us?
Just a stranger on a bus, trying to make His way home . . . [1]

Humanity has long been intrigued at the thought of incarnation, as can be seen in the plaintive lyrics of this popular song. *What if God was one of us?* is a common conundrum posed by mortals who in grappling with the mystery of God end up reducing Him to something manageable, like a stranger on a bus.

For the Christian, the incarnation is the very centerpiece of our faith. God became the *Son of Man*—flesh and blood, bones and joints, muscle and sinew—in order to dwell among us. Yet even we are prone to take such a thing lightly, running the risk of missing eternity's most glorious mystery as we relegate Christ to some position only slightly above fallen man. Our greatest hope for maintaining the holy reverence of which the God-man Christ Jesus is worthy is to ponder His coming to earth within the context of the lofty heights of grandeur He left behind.

Daniel Fuller paints a picture of the incarnation as a winding staircase stretching from the glory of heaven to the world of wretched misery. Upon this staircase, "the length of which cannot be exaggerated, since it spanned the infinite distance between the Creator and the creature," Jesus descends in step after excruciating step. [2] Though His eternal descent had its inception long before the foundation of the world, our first glimpse of it is in a stable reeking of animal dung and moldy straw, where a newborn babe shivering in the chill of night lies vulnerable to the worst conditions humanity has to offer.

From a human standpoint, one could say Jesus never really recovered from that inglorious birth. Soon on the run for their lives, His parents became vagabonds settling as strangers in a foreign land, their very livelihood dependent upon Egyptians, some of whom detested them. Later Mary and Joseph would establish their family in Nazareth, a place of derision even among the Jews for its lack of any distinguishing mark. The descent from glory continued for the *Son of Man* as he grew up in disheartening obscurity, esteemed by none.

Pain permeated Jesus' adult life as well. When fasting in the wilderness to launch His ministry, Satan flaunted His former glory in His face, reminding Him of what He'd left behind. Then for three years the homeless *Son of Man* walked and worked while sleeping in fields and hills, dependent upon benevolent women for financial support, crying out to His Father into the wee hours of His dark and lonely nights. Scorned by heathens, rejected by the religious elite, living under constant threat of death, the descent from glory continued.

Jesus often warned His disciples that the *Son of Man* would suffer many things, as if the dread of what was to come plagued His human heart continually. We only dimly comprehend His true agony as we ponder it in retrospect. Betrayed, arrested, mocked, spat upon, slapped, disdained, and derided, the descent continued. Scourged to a bloody pulp with barely the strength to hang on, burdened with the weight of His own crossbeam and paraded through the streets like a criminal, the descent continued.

Down and down and down the winding staircase Jesus went as He was denied and abandoned by His closest followers and forced to watch His earthly mother mourn in despair. Then for six horrific hours on Calvary, in torture no human mind could possibly conceive, the *Son of Man* descended to the very depths of depravity as He took on the sins of the world. Surely no greater suffering has ever been known than when the King of Glory plunged into that black chasm of alienation from His Father, who'd deserted Him unto death.

This is only a smattering of what it meant for God to become the *Son of Man*. The insidious depths of His descent from glory will perhaps be understood only when we see Him one day on His throne, radiant in splendor, attended by angels and worshiped by saints from every tribe and tongue. Until then, we must ponder often the wonder of the Incarnation.

When we consider the conditions to which Jesus submitted himself in order to secure redemption for our souls, we can only exclaim, "O God, how great a salvation!" And when we find ourselves distraught by our inadequate lives and discouraged by our bumbling attempts to please Him, we need only contemplate that infinite staircase upon which our Lord descended. In this we find hope and receive assurance that God will do everything necessary to accomplish His work in our hearts by His grace and for His glory. *What then shall we say to these things? If God is for us, who is against us? He who did not spare His own Son, but delivered Him up for us all, how will He not also with Him freely give us all things?* (Romans 8:31–32).

RESPOND

The reality that Christ, second person of the triune Godhead, emptied himself of glory to dwell among men is a truth that must never be treated lightly. Spend some time today meditating upon His life. Read back through the devotional, asking God to fill you with a sense of what Jesus must have experienced. Consider that His entire life was one of grief, sorrow, rejection, and derision. He was an outcast in every way and must have felt it keenly all His life. Worship Him, offering a heart of thanksgiving and praise.

Scripture says that the Son of Man, who was inordinately wealthy, became a beggar so that through His complete poverty we might gain wealth. This is the mystery of the Incarnation. What are some of the things that comprise the wealth He gained for you through His poverty? Ponder this and write a prayer of response.

A Prayer

O my Lord, what can it mean that you became one of us? How does the Almighty God manage the loss of glory? Were you terrified to shed heaven's splendor and fall down, down, down to dwell among earth's depraved denizens? What was it like to be a beggar at man's mercy, tempted in every way but not sinning, learning lessons of obedience by suffering? This is simply something I cannot fathom, my Lord. My heart yearns with desire to worship in some way worthy of all you've done. I come with nothing, my Lord, and yet everything, for through your poverty I have been made rich. I love you, and there is nothing else to say, O precious Son of Man.

HEIR

Inheritor, Beneficiary, Successor, Possessor, Recipient

REFLECT

Open your heart to God as you wait before Him today. Ask Him to meet you, to speak to you and reveal His perspective. Consider for a moment the brevity of your life. Whether one believes the world is thousands or billions of years old, our time on the earth is only a breath. In contrast, the triune God has no beginning and will have no end. Jesus is both antecedent and subsequent to every iota of life on this planet. Ponder this as you read Psalm 93 aloud, offering it as praise to Him.

READ

Choose at least two of the following passages to read carefully, asking the Spirit of God to speak: Psalm 22:27; Psalm 2:7–8; Psalm 111:6; Hebrews 1:1–2; Revelation 5:9; Matthew 28:19. Then read the following devotional.

> *God . . . in these last days has spoken to us in His Son, whom He appointed heir of all things, through whom also He made the world.*
>
> HEBREWS 1:1–2

Today . . . this very moment . . . a scene so delightful, so glorious that a glimpse of it would send our souls into orbit, is unfolding in a spiritual realm known as the *third heaven*. A drama of epic proportions involving the destiny of every believer in Christ, this event is more real than the physical world we can see and touch and smell. It is the fulfillment of an agenda the triune God established before the foundation of the world and should thus captivate and enthrall our hearts.

What is it? It is the throne room of the living God, a spiritual splendor where the supremacy of Jesus Christ in His infinite and transcendent beauty is fully manifested. Throughout Scripture we see fragments of what this looks like in something called *theophanies,* encounters with God where our spiritual eyes are opened to see for brief seconds eternity in all its glory.

Moses and the elders were awed by the feet of God resting on a pavement of brilliant sapphire stones in an eternal expanse as clear as the heavens. Isaiah was undone as the quaking temple filled with smoke while flaming six-winged seraphim cried out in antiphonal chorus. Ezekiel's vision of a fire-cloud spewing lightning flashes, and Daniel's river, ablaze as it flowed from the Ancient of Days, boggles the mind. Paul was not even allowed to reveal the *inexpressible words* he heard when he was taken up into the third heaven.[1]

Though fire-clouds and flaming seraphim strain our finite imaginations, something of far greater magnificence moves the heart of Almighty God as He takes in the grand scene around His throne. It is the inheritance He granted His Son before the foundation of the world. The prophets foretold it, Jesus lived and died to gain it, and His final words on earth were a mandate for us to be a part of bringing it about. John's vision resounds with the glory of it:

> *After these things I looked, and behold, a great multitude, which no one could count, from every nation and all tribes and peoples and tongues, standing before the throne and before the Lamb, clothed in white robes, and palm branches were in their hands.* (Revelation 7:9)

When God the Father made His Son the *Heir* of all things, Jesus became the desire of the nations, guaranteeing that believers from every tribe and tongue would one day worship at His feet. This is the joy that was set before Him, the ecstasy He envisioned when sweating drops of blood, stumbling down the Via Dolorosa, and groaning on Calvary's tree. As a result of His suffering, the Father delights to present to His *Heir* a kaleidoscope of worshiping saints whose hearts have been made new through the gift of redemption.

This is the wonder that captivated a small group of Moravian refugees one night in 1727 when the Spirit of God fell upon their chapel services. As revival fires burned through their midst, they became enthralled with the crucified Christ and set out to "win for the Lamb the reward of His sufferings."[2] The small commune of three hundred soon began a twenty-four-hour-a-day prayer meeting for souls, which was sustained for one hundred years.

In the three decades following this amazing move of God, the Moravians "carried the Gospel of salvation by the blood of the Lamb not only to nearly every country in Europe but also to many pagan races in North and South America, Asia, and Africa."[3] History reveals that in twenty years they initiated more mission endeavors than the whole evangelical church had done in two centuries.

And the cause cannot but continue until the whole world knows, for "all of history is moving toward one great goal, the white-hot worship of God and his Son among all the peoples of the earth."[4] God's agenda is a global one—indeed, Jesus promised that once every tongue and tribe has heard, the end of this world as we know it will come (Matthew 24:14). Until then, the Father grants to all His Son's followers the glorious privilege of participating in securing His inheritance, winning the reward for His suffering on Calvary. The wonder of this—that one day we might lay at Christ's nail-scarred feet a crown of souls bought by His own blood—ought to cause our hearts to tremble and to fill us with desire to daily take up our cross in pursuit of that goal.

Let us press on with all our might, scorning the treasures of this world, enduring *all things for the sake of those who are chosen, that they also may obtain the salvation which is in Christ Jesus and with it eternal glory* (2 Timothy 2:10). May we live for the moment when we too will join that symphony of praise, chorus of cultures, panoply of colors, and torrent of tongues who bring delight to the Father as we worship Jesus, the *Heir,* who died to make us His inheritance.

RESPOND

The triune God determined even before the foundation of the world to bring people from every ethnic group[5] into a saving relationship with Him that they might one day enjoy together His glorious presence and worship at His feet. This is seen throughout Scripture and mandated in Jesus' final words—the Great Commission. How might an emphasis on Jesus as our *personal Savior* keep us from embracing this?

Since Scripture guarantees that there *will* be a day when every tribe and tongue will worship Jesus, why do you think God has chosen to accomplish the task of spreading the Good News through us? In what ways are you participating in God's global agenda to secure His Son's inheritance? Praying? Giving? Going? Sending? Proclaiming?

As followers of Christ who have been transformed by His saving blood, the Father longs to fulfill our deepest desires for joy by allowing us to *win for the Lamb the reward of His suffering*. How might this perspective change the way you approach every aspect of your life? Consider this and write a prayer of response.

A Prayer

O Lord, you alone are Heir, for no one else is worthy. How I long for you to receive the reward of your suffering. I see you hanging from Golgotha's tree and wonder if you heard that colossal chorus of praise in every conceivable language echoing like thunder from your throne. I feel as if I can almost hear it now—a cacophony of delightful worship—and I want to run to the nations until all have heard and you come to claim your inheritance. Stir me today, O glorious Heir of all things, that I might ever live for the joy of that majestic moment.

TEACHER

Master, Trainer, Guide, Instructor, Tutor, Mentor

DAY EIGHT

REFLECT

Today as you enter this time of prayer, see yourself as a student sitting at the feet of a great Master. Ready your heart just as you would ready your paper and pen if you were in a college class. Ask the Holy Spirit to gather your thoughts, to bring all your attention to bear on this session with your beloved Teacher, Jesus Christ. Offer Him your undivided attention, asking for the power to seek His face and hear His voice. Express the yearning of your heart to go beyond head knowledge to heart-transforming revelation.

READ

Choose one or more of the following passages: John 3:2; John 13:13; Psalm 25:4–5; Psalm 143:10; Luke 6:40; Colossians 3:10. Read them, asking the Holy Spirit to impart something fresh to you as you do. Then read the following devotional.

A pupil is not above his teacher; but everyone, after he has been fully trained, will be like his teacher.

LUKE 6:40

In the waning years of the twentieth century, we as American Christians seemed oddly inclined to characterize our beliefs in simple slogans and evangelically correct icons. From T-shirts to bumper stickers, bracelets to bedspreads, screen-savers to billboards, we felt the need, as believers living in a post-Christian culture, to brandish the tenets of our faith. To an outside observer, navigating the waters of our religion might have seemed as simple as posting the latest catch phrase like sacred graffiti on our wrists or Web sites or living room walls.

One popular example was *WWJD,* a code reminding believers to ask *What Would Jesus Do?* before they took any action or made any decision. The idea most likely came from Charles Sheldon's book *In His Steps,* a nineteenth-century classic about what happened to a small town when a group of believers engaged in an experiment to base their entire lives on the actions of Christ for one year.

In a review of that book (newly revised) on *Amazon.com,* Mrs. B. Dawkins-Shoope from Toledo, Ohio, wrote the following:

> I read the book and tried to follow the reasoning in my personal life. For instance, when trying to decide between two Ralph Lauren polo shirts—one a celedon green and one a melon—I stopped to consider what Jesus would do, and then bought the melon-colored shirt. But when I got home and put it on I looked SO washed out. Jesus had a swarthy Mediterranean complexion, which was complemented by shades in the orange family. I, however, am of Norse descent, and the melon looked horrible on me. Even though it doesn't really cover it in the book, I'm convinced that you have to think, WWJWFM? or "What Would Jesus Want For Me?" But I guess that's too much for a bracelet or a bumper sticker. Thanks, anyway.

Though surely Mrs. Dawkins-Shoope's review was tongue-in-cheek, it demonstrates well the difficulties of fad and trinket theology. God is incomprehensible, and the faith He instills resonates with infinite awe, ever resisting reduction to the common denominator of the day. However happy and wholesome the outcome of living by *WWJD*, God's purpose for the elect is far more profound. Jesus came, lived, died, and rose again to display the glory of His Father, and His purpose for our lives is the same. This goes far beyond memorizing or mimicking His behavior, for such efforts in and of themselves are destined to fall short, to lack the glory of God.

But if doing what Jesus did doesn't necessarily display God's glory, then what does? How do we live in such a way that the beauty of His Being is reflected in all we are and do? Jesus gives us some insight in one of His discussions with the disciples. He explains to them that through His unique relationship to them as *Teacher*, they would gain something greater than instruction, for not only would they *act* like Him but they would also *be* like Him. In other words, to sit at His feet would mean to undergo a transformation so intense as to conform them to His image from the very core of their being. This is the legacy He left for every true disciple.

How does this happen? The prophet Isaiah notes, *He, your Teacher will no longer hide Himself, but your eyes will behold your Teacher. And your ears will hear a word behind you, "This is the way, walk in it," whenever you turn to the right or to the left* (Isaiah 30:20–21). Truly there is a mystery here and a wonder. Once He was hidden from our darkened hearts, but now our *Teacher* comes by His Spirit, and our eyes behold His beauty. He speaks, and our ears are opened to the voice of heaven while His very Being is branded upon our souls. Everything else flows from this.

Paul said it is in the very act of *beholding* that we are transformed—from one unimaginable glory to another (2 Corinthians

3:18). One pastor has delightfully dubbed this process "transformation by fascination."[1] In absolute awe that we have been given the privileged place of student of the Most High, we are intrigued by every word from His mouth and crave an eternal apprenticeship. We no longer check in with a utilitarian mandate to get a plan for the moment, for our chief joy is in seeing our *Teacher* through the eyes of our heart, knowing we've found at last the secret of living as He lived.

In all fairness, the *WWJD* fad produced some good results. It may have served a little like the law, a tutor reminding people of their desperate need for transforming power to live the Christian life. But the time for a tutor has passed. Jesus the *Teacher* has come, granting grace to be changed from the inside out that we might shine forth with the glory of His greatness. Let us sit joyfully at His feet.

RESPOND

The position of Teacher or Rabbi to the Jews was one of great respect, implying honor and authority. The highest compliment a student could give his teacher was to sit under him in order to become like him in every way. Do you honor Christ by sitting as a student at His feet? Why do you think this glorifies Him more than simply trying to do the things He did?

We are given the unique privilege of living life under the tutelage of Jesus himself. We wait for Him, we behold Him (gaze upon Him), we hear His voice and learn His ways that we might do His will. Have you discovered the joy of this in your own experience? In what ways might you be serving a lesser call, grasping or settling for changes in external behavior?

Ponder the wonder of this amazing reality that Jesus has personally chosen you for His student, given you a place of direct instruction every day and throughout the day. Write a prayer of response.

A Prayer

Teacher, I come to you like an excited child on the first day of school. I am wide-eyed—so much to learn, so much to glean, so much to take in. I look to you in awe that you have chosen me to be your student, to transform me into a bright reflection of your beauty in this battered world. And yet, Lord, I am so easily distracted. In the hustle and bustle of this life, I forget there is a Voice to be heard, a Face to behold, and a Way to discover. I confess, O Teacher, that I may need more than a whisper in my ear. Capture my attention—pierce my preoccupations with the light of your love. Mesmerize me with the sound of your voice. Tutor, mentor, guide, and instruct me, for I yearn to be changed, Jesus, blessed Teacher.

CAPTAIN OF THE HOSTS OF HEAVEN

Commander, Leader, Chief Officer, Authority

REFLECT

As you quiet your heart today, read Psalm 121:1–2. Lift your eyes to the Lord, the Maker of heaven and earth. Let this reality settle in your soul. Offer words of praise for His greatness. Consider the spiritual battles you have faced in the past week. What were some of them? Relational issues? Doubt? Fear? Frustration? Self-condemnation? What did you do? Were you able to identify the attacks against your faith that Satan may have launched? Were you able to draw on Jesus as the Source of victory for these things? Why or why not?

In your prayer journal, write out what you feel is the greatest spiritual battle you face right now. Ask God to speak to your heart concerning it as you continue your time with Him.

READ

Peruse slowly at least two of the following passages, asking God to press their truth into your heart. Follow this by reading the devotional. Nehemiah 9:6; Daniel 4:35; Joshua 5:14–15; Psalm 68:17; Matthew 26:53; Hebrews 1:6–7, 14.

The captain of the Lord's host said to Joshua, "Remove your sandals from your feet, for the place where you are standing is holy."

JOSHUA 5:15

My youngest son, who at fifteen years old is a walking encyclopedia on the military, wars, and weapons, intrigues me. He spends most of his free time watching old war movies, strategizing for virtual combat on the computer, or organizing his collection of military action figures. He's made a hobby of photographing them in battle scenes, giving careful attention to the slightest detail, like the slant of their weapons or the precision of their uniforms.

This tends to give my husband and me great pause, given we own no guns nor have we ever purchased them as toys for our sons. While I tend to fret and try to discourage his quest for military erudition, there is some comfort in knowing that my son, like scores of boys gone before him, is captivated by an age-old theme: the triumph of good over evil. Perhaps this fascination reflects a desire God himself has placed in his heart, a shadow of spiritual reality invisible to the natural eye.

Scripture tells us that in the spiritual realm—beyond the pale of this physical world—powers, principalities, rulers, and authorities wage a war unlike any other, massive in its scope. Though much must be left to the imagination, a few things are clear. Two forces vie for the hearts of men, and though the war was actually won when Christ cried out, *It is finished,* the mop-up operation will continue in earnest until the end of time. Jesus Christ, *Captain of the Hosts of Heaven,* leads His armies in continual assault against Satan and his defeated demons.

What plan is taking place in this heavenly saga? What are the strategies by which the armies of the Evil One will one day face final defeat? A few things are clear. First, like any successful war leader, Jesus our Captain is personally committed to the cause for which He leads His forces. His passion for His Father's glory and His own name drives Him forward with thunderous zeal. Though Satan the thief ever lives to rob, steal, kill, and destroy God's reputation, Jesus' passion to uphold it is stronger. This, He explained to His disciples, would be the impetus behind His answering all prayer in His name *that the Father may be glorified in the Son* (John 14:13).

Second, just as military commanders cannot fight effectively without sanction to lead as they see fit, Jesus Christ answers only to the Father, who has given Him all authority in heaven and on earth, even over Satan and his demons. Because He created them for His own use, Jesus reigns over all that is visible and invisible, over thrones, dominions, rulers, and authorities (Colossians 1:16). Though we do not yet see the full scope of it, when Jesus rose from the dead to be seated at God's right hand, He put all things in subjection under His feet, leaving nothing outside His rule (Hebrews 2:8). Jesus alone has the authority to do what it takes to bring His armies to victory.

Third, troop loyalty is critical for strength in leadership. A captain must be sure that his forces will follow his command. The hosts of heaven—numbering in multiplied millions—bow low before Jesus their *Captain.* They are ministering spirits, at His beck and call to do His bidding. Jesus told the disciples in the Garden of Gethsemane that He could simply appeal to His Father and twelve legions of angels would be instantly at His disposal (Matthew 26:53). Could we but see into the unseen realm, we might be astonished at the glorious victories won daily by Christ's hosts in battle array.

Finally, a military captain must have sufficient firepower to fight to the finish. In one of the most exquisite prophecies in Scripture, Isaiah sees a vision of the crucified Christ that powerfully reveals the nature of His warring spirit: Marching in majestic strength with garments stained by the lifeblood of those He died to redeem, Jesus proclaims—upheld by the Father's wrath—that He trod the wine trough alone, for *the day of vengeance was in My heart, and My year of redemption has come* (Isaiah 63:4).

The firepower against Satan is fueled by nothing less than the wrath of God against sin, the very wrath that Jesus took upon himself in the endless agony of Golgotha. And though the Father did not lift His hand to bring relief during those tortuous moments, a day is coming when He will express the full force of His ire. What the world will witness in that day of vengeance as God vindicates the redemption for which His Son paid so dearly is beyond imagination. The firepower of His fierce wrath will not subside until Satan and his demons have been cast into outer darkness for the rest of eternity.

As followers of Christ, we will be in the thick of battle until the day He calls us home or returns in glorious victory. We have been given an incredible privilege, primarily through prayer, to fight this war and enjoy conquests every day of our lives as we storm the gates of hell. "Our voice may be silent, our lips may not move, but our eye is on our Captain. Our hand is touching His throne. Our faith is raising the banner of the cross. Our soul is shouting the name of Jesus."[1]

With eager anticipation the church of Jesus Christ marches on, for our *Captain* is a sure victor. Heavenly hosts abound, existing for no other purpose than to carry out Christ's plans. May this reality fill us with confidence and stir us with zeal, until we go forth like a mighty army, rejoicing in the hope of that final day when wars cease and our *Captain* reigns in glorious and eternal victory.

RESPOND

Christ, Captain of the multiplied millions of angels who do His bidding, defeated Satan through His death and resurrection. Though a defeated foe, Satan seeks to destroy anything that glorifies God. What kinds of lies do you think he tells you personally in order to accomplish this?

Victory in Christ is ours to the degree that we yield control of our lives to Him. He has the ultimate power and authority over all spiritual authorities to finish the work of the Cross in your own heart. He is the Conqueror in every situation, good or bad. What might change in your life if you were continually aware of this truth? Write a prayer of affirmation based on one of the passages you've read today concerning the battles in your spiritual journey.

A Prayer

Jesus, I confess that I tend to treat the truth of the war in the heavenlies like a fantasy—some kind of sci-fi saga outside my reach. But evil is so very real, and the battle to destroy your holy name screams in the streets, at times ravaging my own soul. You are the victorious warrior and I long to live in that hope. Let me hear your voice commanding the hosts of heaven, proclaiming victories large and small, that I might see the beauty of your glorious reign. Send your ministering spirits to my heart and home, flaming with your fire until the day you lead us to our final triumph, O conquering Captain.

I AM

Self-Existent, Uncreated, Preexistent, Perpetual, Infinite

REFLECT

Today as you come before God, ask Him to open your heart to mysteries you've not understood before. The self-existence of God can be both humbling and awe-inspiring. Spend a few minutes quietly contemplating the reality that He has no beginning and no end. What does this mean to you? How does it impact the way you live your life?

READ

Read a few of the following Scriptures, asking God to capture your heart with the awe His eternal status should inspire. When you have finished, prayerfully read the devotional. Genesis 1:1; Psalm 90:2; Exodus 3:14; Isaiah 43:13; John 8:58; Revelation 22:13.

I am the . . . first and the last,
the beginning and the end.

REVELATION 22:13

The first dramatic dialogue between God and Moses is a feast for the senses, filled with mind-boggling morsels. After getting his attention through blazing bush pyrotechnics and a blast of thunderous voice, God reveals His plan to deliver the Hebrew people from Egyptian bondage using Moses as their fearless leader.

One can almost imagine Moses the meek, bare feet burning, palms sweating, heart pounding, and voice trembling as He ekes out *Who am I?* God quickly dismisses the question as irrelevant in light of the fact that He would be joining him in the venture, to which Moses, with perhaps a tad more boldness, asks, *Well, then— who are You?*[1]

Moses' mindset at the time may reveal the significance of this weighty exchange. Having grown up among the Egyptians, he was familiar with many gods. He knew Heka, the goddess of procreation, and Imhotep, the god of medicine. He was well acquainted with Isis, the goddess of life, and Seth, the protector of crops. He'd grown up with Hapi, guardian of the Nile, and Osiris, giver of life—but who was this God, whose voice bellowed from a burning bush, bestowing such a call on him, a simple sheepherder?

For Moses and the people to whom he would return, everything hinged upon the answer to this question. After four hundred years in captivity, the memory of the God of Abraham, Isaac, and Jacob was surely dim if not completely obliterated for most. Instead, they were familiar with the same gods Moses knew, each one's name representing what it provided—health, fertility, love, riches, lands, protection—in exchange for their service. Without knowing the name of this God he'd so dramatically encountered, Moses had nothing to offer the people to entice them to follow.

God's response was simple and stunning: *"I AM who I AM. Thus you shall say to the sons of Israel, 'I AM has sent me to you'"* (Exodus 3:14).

Perhaps there are some lessons to be learned from this epic

interchange for the church in America today. Clearly, Moses felt that the way to convince the Hebrew people was to bring them a god who would meet them at some point of need, offering gifts that outshone those of other gods. Glancing across the landscape of Christianity today, it seems we are ever prone to make the same mistake. We condense the gospel message to a litany of good things that God is waiting to give. We expound in felt-need sermons, hoping to convince seekers who are looking for the god with the greatest goods. Peace, fulfilling careers, happiness, restored marriages, well-rounded children, health, financial success—God is the vehicle, we imply, just waiting for you and me to get on board.

But the eternal, infinite Essence of Being challenged Moses and us as well to grasp that which makes all these things extraneous. *I AM.* This is the truth He calls each of us to recognize and reckon with and rest in. *I AM who I AM.* God *is.* And because He *is,* we have our being. This is the truth that hundreds of years later Jesus would dangerously flaunt, enraging pious Pharisees who sought to deny His divinity. *"Truly, truly, I say to you, before Abraham was born, I AM."*

In an impenetrable mystery, this God of the burning bush, the great *I AM,* shed His robes of glory to walk among men while retaining His essence as Almighty. Jesus Christ was and is the great *I AM,* the God who cannot change, the Eternal One, who precedes and succeeds us, and from whom we derive the very air we breathe. Yes, He is a rewarder of those who seek Him, but those who seek Him must first believe that *He is* (Hebrews 11:6).

It is an irony that in the end there is only One giver of good and perfect gifts, One who is truly benevolent. There is only One who can give without charge, for He has never had need of man's service to enrich Him. He is complete in every way—full of glory—and throughout Scripture shuns every suggestion of a quid pro quo relationship, every notion that people work for Him in order to earn His blessings.[2]

I AM. This is the foundation, the hinge upon which all else hangs. This thought should plague, astonish, stun, comfort, and enflame our hearts. There is a God, an eternal river of past, present and future—"one unbroken continuum, undiminished, active and strong."[3] Only when we rightly understand this can we begin to live in the freedom and wonder of His gift of salvation and the multitude of accompanying graces. Jesus *is.* Let the beauty of such a fact settle in our souls as we receive from His hands an eternity of joy.

RESPOND

Scripture both begins and ends with the self-existent God who has always been, is now, and always will be. This reality must be the central theme of our thoughts about God and lives devoted to His cause. Consider the tendency to seek the things God might give as more important than God himself. Do you struggle with this? Why or why not?

Do you tend to see your service toward God as a means whereby you can earn the things He offers, or even His favor? What might be wrong with this thinking, given what you have read today? If God doesn't need what you have to offer and doesn't offer His blessings as bribes for your obedience, what should be your motivation to serve Him? Spend some time pondering these questions.

As the "I AM," Jesus transcends all the limitations of time in which we live. As the "I AM," Jesus acts and no one can reverse it. In what ways can this bring you comfort, hope, and encouragement? Consider, and write a prayer of response.

A Prayer

O great and unfathomable I AM, you who have always been—how can I ever grasp such a knowledge? You dwell completely outside of time, while I am driven by seconds and moments and hours and days. You are perpetually behind me, ever before me, and always with me. Lift up my head, O God, to the transcendent wonder of your uncreated existence. Transport me into heavenly realms, where you act and it cannot be reversed. Let me rest in the infinite mystery that no one can thwart your purposes. You are the Center; now come and be the Center of all that I am or think or do, O great I AM.

IMMANUEL

Companion, Ever-Present, Attendant, Resident

REFLECT

Spend a few minutes quietly pondering the reality that God is present, that through His Spirit Jesus has come to dwell within you. Is this something you tend to take for granted? Are you overcome with the mystery of such a thing?

Offer a prayer of gratitude for the miracle of the indwelling Christ. Ask Him to make His presence real in ways you've not yet seen.

READ

Choose one or more of the following passages to read slowly and ponder: Matthew 1:23; Matthew 28:20; John 14:16; Romans 8:11; 2 Corinthians 6:16; Revelation 21:3. When you feel God has spoken, read the devotional that follows.

"And they shall call His name Immanuel," which translated means, "God with us."

MATTHEW 1:23

In his book *God in the Wasteland,* theologian David Wells traces the rise of rationalism in the Western world and its tragic effects on the church in the twentieth century. He suggests that as the culture deified the scientific method, Christians responded by formulating a God who could be understood, measured, explained, and contained. The result was a serious "dumbing down" of spiritual truth.

Wells carefully delineates the process by which the church fashion-fitted God to meet the ever-increasing demands of a consumer culture and pacify the plethora of our psychological needs until what was left was a people "deaf to the summons of the external God. All too often," Wells adds, "he now leans weakly on the church, a passive bystander . . . that is to say, God has become weightless."[1]

A *weightless* God is surely a far cry from the One whose presence once rent the earth to swallow sinners or caused well-worn priests to flee from the cloud-filled temple in holy fear. Sadly for many, the idea of *Immanuel*—the *present* Christ—is little more than an icon—a picture of a throne upon which our Savior sits (or wishes to sit) in the hollow of our hearts.

Yet history is replete with stories of believers whose lives were rocked when their eyes were finally opened to the mystical, supernatural reality that Christ inhabited their very souls. Augustine lamented how he came so late to love this beautiful Jesus, having looked without in vain for that which was within. He wrote:

> You were within me while I was outside of myself. . . . Then you called me and cried to me and broke through my deafness! You sent forth your beam, the light of your magnificently beautiful presence. You shone your Self upon me to drive away my blindness. You breathed your fragrance upon me . . . and in astonishment I drew my breath . . . now I pant for you! I tasted you, and now I hunger and thirst for you. You touched me—and I burn to live within your peace.[2]

How can we explain *Immanuel*—this sense of Someone so real that we find ourselves aligning our entire lives to please Him yet so intangible we will ever fail to find words to describe His worth? *Immanuel* is not an idea, a doctrine, a "ghost of religious fantasy in our minds," or a sentimental fabrication of what seems important to us."[3] The Christ who indwells us by His Spirit is a violent force, ever seeking to destroy the deeds of our flesh and breathe in and through us a life so palpable that we could never doubt that He has come.

The reality that El Shaddai, Elohim, the God of Abraham, Isaac, and Jacob, the first and last, King of Kings and Lord of Lords has come—not only to redeem but to indwell us—should turn our world upside down. He is the external God: Nothing we do or think can change the slightest facet of His glory. No one can ward off His hand or say to Him, "What have you done?" for He is in the heavens and He does whatever He pleases (Daniel 4:35). But oh, what a wonder: He is *Immanuel,* God with us.

Let us pray that the weight of this God might fall once again, that we would lie prostrate at His feet, crying out for grace to set us free from banal beliefs. Surely Christ beckons us to repent of hearts that see Him so small we think our works enrich Him, our programs support Him, and our lives are indispensable to His plan.

To see Him move and work in power for His name's sake must become our consuming passion, deepening and intensifying as His Spirit takes control of our hearts. Let us settle for nothing less than the explosive inhabitation of the living Lord so that our children, our neighbors, our co-workers, and, yes, the nations may know at last that *Immanuel* has come.

RESPOND

God is with us. This is not merely an idea but a full spiritual reality. Jesus has come to us, revealing the mystery planned before the world began, to put His Spirit within us that we might know Him and glorify Him. Why do you think people tend to take this lightly or fail to see the awe of it? What has the indwelling Christ meant to you personally? How real is His presence in your day-to-day living of life?

That God is with us—that He indwells us by His Spirit—should stun us once we truly see it with spiritual eyes. Stop and consider His name: *Immanuel.* Muse on it, ponder it, and ask the very Spirit of Christ who lives within you to reveal the wonder of this. Wait in awe-filled silence before Him.

A Prayer

O precious Immanuel, how can I ever truly appreciate the mystery that you have come to me? God with us—in me, and around me, and within me—the very air I breathe. What have we missed, Immanuel? Why does your indwelling presence not explode in power, changing our hearts and the world in which we live? How we need you to come in a fresh way, to show us the unsettling mystery that the living God dwells within our souls. O Immanuel, bear down upon me with a weight I cannot resist. Stir within me with zeal I never dreamed possible. Then I will live for your fame, then I will see your kingdom come, then the cry of my heart on the highways and byways will ever be, "O come, O come, Immanuel."

THE DOOR

Entrance, Gateway, Opening, Access, Passageway

REFLECT

Welcome God's presence as you come to Him today. Take some time to acknowledge that your desire is to encounter Him, to hear His voice and know His heart. Imagine for a moment the doors that you go through on any given day. What do they lead to? What would happen if they suddenly closed and you couldn't use them anymore?

Ponder the warning Jesus seeks to give when He speaks of himself as the narrow door many will never go through. Consider the seriousness of His teaching that one day the door to salvation will be shut forever. Ponder your salvation and pray for those who don't yet know Him. Write specific requests for at least one lost person who has not yet entered the Door of Jesus.

READ

Read a few of the following verses and the devotional provided: Matthew 16:24–25; John 10:9; Matthew 7:13–14; Psalm 118:19–20.

Strive to enter by the narrow door; for many, I tell you, will seek to enter and will not be able.

LUKE 13:24

In 1993 the Jesus Seminar[1] released its long-touted *The Five Gospels: The Search for the Authentic Words of Jesus,* raising the eyebrows and ire of many conservative Christians. The book unveiled the results of a series of meetings in which scholars, having done extensive research, cast their votes on purported sayings of Jesus. This they did by dropping a bead in a box, the color of which reflected the degree of authenticity they felt the words had.

In its final analysis, the Jesus Seminar claimed to have confidence in only 18 percent of the sayings Scripture attributes to Jesus. All else was deemed unreliable and/or fictitious. A closer look at their results revealed that the study's foundational assumptions denied divine inspiration, making their task simply one of compiling data based on human reasoning and research.

For those of us who view Scripture as the sacred Word of God, the thought of men emasculating it by casting colored beads seems an arrogance of the worst sort. I remember my own distaste when I read of their findings. And yet as I looked further, there was something about the honesty in their approach that bothered me and then brought conviction. I found myself thinking that though I say I believe that every word of Scripture is God-breathed, I too cast my own colored beads simply by ignoring those words of Jesus that don't fit with my way of life. The participants in the Jesus Seminar with their liberal bent toward Scripture may be more authentic in their disbelief than those of us who profess beliefs our actions belie.

What are we to do with the hard sayings of Jesus? Do we grapple with His mandate to love Him so fiercely that familial love looks like hate in comparison? Are we wrestling with what He meant when He commanded us not to store up treasures on earth? To give away all our possessions? Would He call us fools for our stock portfolios and houses and retirement plans? Do we love our enemies, give our coat to the one who sues for our shirt, keep our spiritual achievements private, and look for ways to serve others rather than lead them? Will we forgive our brother as often as he sins against us? Is the driving passion of our days to go into all the world and make disciples?[2]

Even as I write these things my heart struggles, for I'm not sure what this kind of life looks like. I tend to assume that people like Hudson Taylor or William Carey or Amy Carmichael were somehow uniquely chosen, saints with a special calling. Could this be how I and others like me have cast our colored beads—voting yes on Jesus' kind, saving words for ourselves and assuming those more difficult and demanding apply to someone else? Surely such an approach to the Christian faith dishonors God, for it makes us our own little sovereigns, choosing what and when and how to obey.

When Jesus claimed to be the *Door,* He spoke soberly of a singular entrance to eternal life. Few will find it, He warned, though many will try. He cautions by way of parable that in the end He will close the *Door,* leaving untold millions to an eternity of destruction outside His presence. He warns us that many of those left without will be ones who claimed to follow Him, called Him Lord, and even demonstrated powerful works in His name. Is there any more sobering passage in all of Scripture? (Matthew 7:21–23).

So what are we to do? Perhaps we must first seek to understand the nature of the narrow way. *Take up your cross,* Jesus admonished His hearers over and over again, warning them that every other love, including the self-love that fights to maintain our own sovereignty, must fall to the ground like a grain of wheat and die. To enter the gates of eternity requires nothing less than annihilation of our very self, for to follow Christ is to go through a *Door* of death, as He did on Golgotha.

This will never happen through mere discipline and duty. It requires something far more than willpower and fleshly zeal. We must be driven by the reality that this *Door* of death is also a *Door* of life. There is a joy set before us that makes the dying gain, for in plunging us beneath the fountain of His blood, Jesus raises us to a life of delight we can only begin to fathom in this fallen world. When our hearts are set aflame by the wonder that we've entered into the heart of Christ to partake of His very nature, then perhaps we will find the holy passion to follow hard after Him (2 Peter 1:4).

In this life we will always fail to live up to the exacting mandates of Jesus, feeling an ever-increasing awareness of how far we have to go. Yet we must press on: wrestling, working, yielding a bit more with each day. As we come to tremble in awe that the *Door* has been thrown open, perhaps we'll begin to notice that something in us has changed, that we can no longer savor the things of this world. Like the sun slowly dawning on a darkened night, we will see at last that we are gladly giving up our life to find it in the glory of His precious presence.

RESPOND

We are saved and given free access to the very presence of God through the righteousness of Jesus who died that we might live. In taking up our cross we embrace His death in our death and find glorious, abundant life. How have you tended to view Jesus' words about your cross? Have they felt heavy, burdensome? If so, ask Him to begin to reveal the glory that is yours; it will make you want to run to Him with reckless abandon.

The reality of redemption is a rare treasure not to be taken for granted. Jesus is a Door with limited access, and relatively few people ever find the narrow way. Do you live with this awareness? Does it cause you to embrace the hard mandates Christ has given? In what ways are you learning to *take up your cross* for the joy set before you?

We live today in an age of mercy. The Door is still open to all that will come. But a time is coming when the Door will be shut with a terrifying finality. How do you think this reality should impact your thinking? Your daily life? Do you rejoice continually that you have entered through the gate to find free access to the living God? Do you also sense a weight in crying out for the hearts of the lost, being ever aware of the sound of that Door slamming shut for all time? Reflect on these things and write a prayer of response.

A Prayer

Dearest Door to my heart's desire, how I rejoice in the awesome wonder that you have granted me free access into your very presence. I once wandered about like an unkempt beggar outside the gate, ravenously hungry, while the scent of your glory wafted in the distance. Then one day you threw open the Door, dressed me in glorious robes of your own righteousness, and beckoned me in to dwell in the shadow of your breathtaking beauty. I adore your presence, Lord, but feel a certain urgency in my soul. So many are still lost outside; millions do not know you've made a way for them to enter in. Stir my heart with the wonder of what you've done, and make me cry out day and night for those lost in darkness who wait for someone to run to them with joy and proclaim that the Door is open for them this very day.

HOPE OF GLORY

Eternal Expectation, Pleasurable Anticipation,
Eager Longing, Joyful Prospect

REFLECT

Begin today by expressing your heart toward God concerning the blessings of your salvation. Meditate upon 1 Peter 1:3–5, phrase by phrase, offering words of worship in response as you go. (To meditate, ask the Holy Spirit to reveal truth as you ponder questions such as: What does this mean? What does this say about God? What does this say about my life? Ask, *Lord, what do you want me to know, to understand, to embrace, to do as a result of this truth?*)

READ

Choose two or more of the following passages to consider. Read them aloud once or twice, then read the devotional that follows. Colossians 1:27; Psalm 16:11; Titus 2:13; 2 Timothy 2:10; 1 Corinthians 2:7; Ephesians 1:18.

Christ in you, the hope of glory.

COLOSSIANS 1:27

They were a normal missionary family, traveling by houseboat up and down the Amazon River to bring the gospel and humanitarian aid to villages along its banks. One fateful day as they flew home from conducting business in the city, Peruvian narcotics agents began to fire at their small bush plane, mistaking them for drug-runners. One bullet hit both thirty-five-year-old Veronica Bowers and the baby daughter she held, killing them instantly. In a dramatic crash landing on the river, her husband, Jim, their seven-year-old son, Corey, and the plane's pilot somehow survived.

Amid the political finger-pointing and massive international publicity, the quiet faith of Jim Bowers sparkled like a precious jewel from the ash heap of grief. In one interview with a major TV network, the host struggled to understand how Jim could be at such peace under the circumstances. Finally, with obvious incredulity, she asked how he could have faith in a God who would take a baby's life. Jim responded: "I have an easy answer, even though I don't understand most of what God does. The real life isn't here on earth. There's going to be billions of years—that's the real life. She had her little seven months here, and now she's with Him in eternity, in perfection."

With those simple words, Jim Bowers articulated a truth concerning a mystery the Bible calls our *Hope of Glory*. The Greek word for *hope* literally means *to anticipate with pleasure*,[1] affirming that those who experience the glory of Christ on this earth will live with joyful expectation of what is to come. That Christ dwells within our hearts by His Spirit will fill us with purpose so profound that we can endure suffering with joy and find hope even in a baby's death.

Paul saw this as his lot in life, having been warned by Jesus from the start of the many things he would suffer for the sake of His name (Acts 9:15–16). But instead of fatalistic resignation or bitter resistance, Paul received it as a gift, challenging Timothy to join him in the holy calling of suffering for Christ (2 Timothy 1:8). After years of every imaginable form of physical, emotional, and spiritual torment, Paul concluded that what he'd experienced wasn't even worthy to be compared to the glory that would be revealed one day (Romans 8:18).

Peter wrote of the inheritance reserved for believers, challenging them to rejoice in suffering, knowing that through it their faith would be perfected, resulting in praise, glory, and honor at the revelation of Jesus Christ. He described his feelings about that day as *joy inexpressible and full of glory* (1 Peter 1:7–8). These and millions of others who have suffered for Christ throughout Christian history testify by their lives that they have tasted of something so glorious, so wonderful, that it is worth losing everything for.

The *Hope of Glory* within ever reminds us that this short season we call life is only a prelude to that moment when every knee will bow before the beauty of this One who has saved our souls. This is the wonder that wakes us each morning with expectation and hope, even amid the darkest hours of our humanity. Because Jesus is our destiny, once we taste of Him, the glory that lies ahead becomes for us the *real life*.

Steve Saint, whose father was killed bringing the gospel to the Auca Indians some forty years ago, spoke at the memorial service for Veronica and Charity Bowers. Addressing his words to young Corey, he reminisced over the funeral for his own father. Remembering conversations with his mom as she tried to explain that his dad would never come home again, he shared:

> So, I asked her, "Where did my dad go?" And she said, "He went to live with Jesus." And you know, that's where my mom and dad had told me that we all wanted to go and live.

Well, I thought, isn't that great that Daddy got to go sooner than the rest of us? And you know what? Now when people say, "That was a tragedy," I know they were wrong.[2]

This mystery—Christ in us, the *Hope of Glory*—transforms every tragedy into a glorious triumph. We live with the pulsing reality that though some go sooner than others, our destiny is a moment when time will be no more, when we will see Jesus face-to-face, when anticipation will be at last eternal fulfillment. What a day, a glorious day, that will be.

RESPOND

Every redeemed soul is indwelt by the presence of Christ through His Spirit, who desires to fill them with joyful anticipation of what is to come, both now and in eternity. This is the hope of glory. How does your life demonstrate that your hope lies not in this life but in eternity? Would those who observe the decisions you make about time, money, possessions, and relationships assume that you are living for this world or the one to come? Why?

Heaven is the real life, this earth only a temporary journey. That we might know the hope of this calling was Paul's prayer for us. We will long for eternity and translate all our experiences in light of that longing to the degree to which we have tasted of the glorious Christ on earth. Have you learned how to taste and see that He is good? Does your life reflect the spiritual discipline of prayer, of drinking from the well of His presence as your continual source? Ponder this and write a response.

A Prayer

O Hope of Glory, you have filled my soul with delight and I find myself daily craving more. I long to know you, to see you, to taste of your goodness and then proclaim your worth to this superficial world so caught up in its temporal treasures. I wonder why, in the light of your glory, I ever settle for lesser things. How is it that this life can so consume me when I am headed for eternity with you? When I am only a vapor, while you are forever? Draw me, O Hope of Glory, to the place where I can see your beauty and live with a holy desire to see it exalted. Let the riches of my inheritance in glory explode within until, filled with pleasurable anticipation of eternity, I forget the past and press on toward you, my precious Jesus.

JUDGE

Arbiter, Magistrate, Adjudicator, Convictor

REFLECT

As you settle into your time with the Lord today, reflect on the reality that when you meet with God, you bring only a willing heart (or even a heart that wants to be made willing). You do not come to "do," to achieve, or to accomplish any agenda. You are here to drink from the Living Fountain and, in drinking, find deep, abiding satisfaction. This is what brings glory to God—your absolute joy and rest in His all-sufficient grace.

Ask the Holy Spirit to show you the things you need to leave behind, the agendas, the works, the efforts to commend yourself to God or others. Come empty and open-handed. Sit for a few minutes in silence with your palms open on your lap. Thank God that His invitation to "Come" is always open.

READ

Choose three or four of the following passages to ponder before you read the devotional. As you read them, ask the Holy Spirit to illumine your heart today to the beauty of Jesus as Judge. Acts 10:42; Matthew 25:31–32; 2 Corinthians 5:10; Revelation 20:11–12; John 5:26–27; Acts 17:30–31.

He gave Him authority to execute judgment,
because He is the Son of Man.

JOHN 5:27

On June 11, 2001, a felon named Timothy McVeigh was executed by lethal injection. Having been convicted of killing 168 people by blowing up an Oklahoma City government building, McVeigh's final words held no plea for forgiveness or whisper of remorse. Instead, he recited a famous poem that ends with this declaration:

And yet the menace of the years
Finds, and shall find, me unafraid.
It matters not how strait the gate,
How charged with punishments the scroll,
I am the master of my fate:
I am the captain of my soul.[1]

Though these chilling lines with which McVeigh chose to exit this world may ring with bravado right now, they will one day dissipate like ashes in the wind, as will all the deception of man concerning human sovereignty. Whether one fears death or not has no bearing on the reality that the omnipotent, omniscient, self-existent God has set in antiquity a day in which to judge the world, a thought that ought to make any mortal tremble.

On that Day of Judgment, every thought and deed will be brought to light and every sin called to account. Every evil act will be vindicated, every wrong made right, every inequity brought into balance, and every heart humbled before the all-seeing God. No one will escape that moment in which rich and poor, old and young, scholar and simpleton, religious and rebellious, powerful and impotent, pompous and meek, will stand beneath the fiery gaze of the one true God to give an account of their life.

There is a judgment to come, for there is a *Judge.* Even now, the exalted Christ sits upon a great white throne awaiting the time appointed by the Father. He alone is worthy to determine the fate of every person, for He is perfect in all His ways, without guile, hypocrisy, or unrighteousness. Jesus is an impartial *Judge,* having neither a hidden agenda nor a personal grudge, for when He shed His own blood on the cross of Calvary He settled sin's score once and for all.

Jesus is a powerful *Judge,* for He rose from the dead, defeating death and its dark forces. When revealed from heaven with His mighty angels in flaming fire, He will deal out retribution to those not cleansed by His blood, demonstrating at last the justice due His holy perfection (2 Thessalonians 1:7–8). From the purity of His presence the very heavens and earth will be forced to flee (Revelation 20:11).

On that day when Jesus separates the sheep from the goats, some will find too late that it is a terrifying thing to fall into the hands of the living God. Every person will look upon Him whom they pierced and will mourn (Revelation 1:7). Men like Timothy McVeigh will see with dread that man is no longer master of his fate or captain of his soul. Many, after bowing their knee and confessing that Jesus Christ is Lord, will face the awful agony of eternity in hell.

But for those whose debt of sin has been paid at the Cross, that "last tremendous day shall dawn with splendor and delight, and not with gloom and terror."[2] There before His throne they too will kneel in awe, listening to the voice of the glorious *Judge* as He declares their innocence. Hear it and tremble with joy, even now. *Come, you who are blessed of My Father, inherit the kingdom prepared for you from the foundation of the world* (Matthew 25:34).

Respond

Though this world is filled with injustice and evil, there is coming a day when everything will be made right through the judgment of Jesus Christ. The punishment for every sin that is not covered by His blood will be imposed in hell. How might this reality affect the way you view the Cross? The events of your life? Your world?

Jesus the Judge will examine every person who has ever lived. Under the glorious gaze of our holy Lord, we will give account for our lives. As His children, though our deeds do not save us, we will be judged by them, for they are the evidence that we've been truly transformed by the grace of God. In what ways do you see this evidence growing in your own heart and life? Ponder this, prayerfully examine your own heart, and write a prayer of response.

A Prayer

O glorious and righteous Judge, that you know my deepest thoughts causes me both to tremble and to rejoice, for though not a day goes by that I don't grieve at my weakness and mourn over my sin, you alone know the longings in my deepest being. You know, O Judge, I want nothing more than to bring you glory, though at times the frailty of my flesh belies such a thing. You know how I ache with love for your name and live to see it exalted, even though my best efforts seem like hay and stubble. But I can only plead both now and in that final judgment that it is your blood that covers me, for without it I would have no hope. Remind me today and every day, Judge of my heart, that only through Calvary can I ever hope to find favor in your sight. All is from you and through you and to you forever. Amen.

RESURRECTION

Reawakener, Revitalizer, Resuscitator

REFLECT

Quietly reflect on the person of Jesus Christ today. What new things have you seen of Him recently? Who is He? Are you learning to regularly ask this question when you come to pray? Read Psalm 27:4 to see how David felt about this process. Is this the one thing you desire?

What thoughts come to mind when you think of the word *resurrection*? Jesus said He *is* the resurrection. This is not only an action but an identity, not just something He did but something He is. What does this mean to you?

READ

Read some of the following Scriptures and the devotional: John 11:25–26; John 6:40; Philippians 3:20–21; Philippians 1:21; John 5:26–29.

I am the resurrection and the life.

JOHN 11:25

Some ten years ago I decided to prepare for our upcoming Easter celebration by meditating in my morning prayer time on Jesus' final hours. Each day I pondered small snippets of Scripture and wrote a prayer of response to the crucified Christ who lives within my soul. Little did I know when I started that I was embarking on a journey that would take more than a year and dramatically impact my spiritual life.

A few years later the opportunity arose to turn those prayer journals into a book that might lead others on their own journey to Calvary.[1] Never have I faced a more difficult writing assignment, before or since. Day after day I sat at my computer as the agony of the Cross consumed my heart. Trying over and over again to delve into the grim depths of Christ's final moments became for me a personal crucifixion.

I saw the humility of the Lord as Jewish leaders jabbed and spat upon Him, and I was undone at my pride. I surveyed the torture inflicted on His body in the scourging alone and was disconcerted by the weakness of my resolve. I watched the courage of Mary, His mother, and John, His friend, and was ashamed at my nonchalance. I saw the cup from which Jesus yearned to be delivered and glimpsed for perhaps a second the wretchedness of my own depravity swirling in its depths.

With every day my depression grew, and at times I could do nothing but weep and wait upon God for strength to write once again. Even now the memories flood my heart with a familiar ache. What relief I felt the day I completed my final editing of the manuscript and sent it off.

A few days later my editor called to express concern over the final chapter on the Resurrection, which I'd written rather hurriedly. He encouraged me to revisit the subject, suggesting that the exhilaration of that event simply did not come through in my writing. He wondered if perhaps my own journey through the pain of the Cross had kept me from experiencing the radical joy of the *Resurrection*.

He was right. As I began to contemplate those moments and the people to whom the risen Christ appeared, a wonderful thing happened. The great weight of the crucifixion lifted, and it seemed as if life was seeping back into my veins once again. I felt a little like Mary, who must have danced through the streets crying out to anyone who would listen: "I have seen the Lord!" I began to grasp that the galling glory of Christ's death takes on breathtaking hues when viewed through the shimmering prism of the *Resurrection*.

Imagine for a moment: Long has earth lain captive under the curse of death. The glory with which God intended to cover her orb seems forever hidden from view. Men and women, once created in His image to shine forth like beaming beacons, bear instead the image of the earthy—depraved and driven by self-love and sin. Groaning under the weight of this evil darkness, all of creation cries out for relief. Arrogant demons flaunt their freedom, wallowing in the hopelessness that permeates the ranks of humanity. It seems as if Satan, stretching forth the tentacles of his limited power, holds the whole world in his grip.

At no time is this more keenly felt than as Christ's body is left to rot in earth's most desolate tomb. Those who had staked their future on His promise of life now seem of all people most to be pitied. And yet . . . *all is not as it seems. While disheartened followers grieve and Pharisees breathe sighs of relief, the Spirit of Christ moves throughout the cosmos, crashing through Hades' gates to proclaim victory over sin and death. In the pit of hell, fallen angels rage at the Son of God who lives after all.*[2]

I am the Resurrection! Jesus sings as He dances into eternity bestowing hope and healing and life everlasting. By one man death had come, and by one man life now reigns. Never has the world seen such a display of power. Never has religion aspired to such heights, for all of humanity's heroes are no more, swallowed up in death, ashes to ashes and dust to dust. But Christ is alive! Once again the earth will shine with His glory. Sinners will be raised to walk in newness of life, bearing at last the heavenly image.

A day is coming when all who dwell on earth's shores will feel the atmosphere shake as Jesus, firstborn from the dead, returns, shattering the sky with a spectacular shout. *Resurrection!* The voice of an archangel ... the trumpet of God ... and time will be no more. *Then we who are alive and remain shall be caught up together with them in the clouds to meet the Lord in the air, and thus we shall always be with the Lord* (1 Thessalonians 4:17). Awesome mystery, glorious ecstasy, *Resurrection!*

RESPOND

God created us in His image that He might fill the earth with His glory. What we gain through Christ's resurrection is newness of life, the capacity once again to bear Christ's image to a world that has not yet seen or known Him. This is the reason for our salvation, the purpose for our time left on this earth. In what ways are you living your life that shines forth the beauty of Christ's image? Do you live to see others have what He has given you? If so, how? If not, what do you think might be missing?

John tells us that when we see Jesus in eternity, we will immediately be like Him (1 John 3:2–3). While we remain on this earth, we become conformed to His image little by little as we behold His glory. It may seem a little dark, like an old mirror, but as we learn to gaze intently, we will be transformed (2 Corinthians 3:18). This is His plan—in what ways are you participating? Often we think we are changed by actions we take, but actions are always to be an overflow of joy from having our souls satisfied in Jesus. Consider this and write a prayer of response.

A Prayer

O Resurrection and Life, how hope fills my soul. Even now the words He is not here, He is risen! *electrify me. I am awestruck that I will spend eternity in your presence, raised by the same power that catapulted you from the dark bowels of the earth into the light of glory. I find myself wanting to dance and sing, to run through the streets as Mary did. O Lord, truly, to live is you and to die is to gain you in your fullness. I cry out for resurrection power even now. Raise my heart to your throne, O God. Raise my eyes to the glory of your name, raise my affections to the level of your worth, flood this frail flesh with life that I might know you and be transformed.*

BRIDEGROOM

Lover, Betrothed, Suitor, Wooer, Promised One

REFLECT

As you prepare your heart to meet with God today, consider what it is like to be a bride eager to commune with her beloved. This is the kind of intimacy Jesus desires to have with you. Ask Him to purify your heart, to make you ready for an exchange of love and a deeper desire for prayer. Offer Him your heart with a sense of joyful abandonment.

READ

Read some of the following passages and jot down thoughts that rise within you. Ask the Holy Spirit to reveal new insights as you read them and the devotional that follows. Matthew 25:5–6; Matthew 9:15; Joel 1:8; Revelation 19:7; Revelation 22:17.

Behold, the bridegroom! Come out to meet him.

MATTHEW 25:6

Her name was Anna, and she was the talk of the town. First there was that temple insanity. Day in and day out she'd practically lived there for as long as anyone could remember. Some claimed her pretense of piety had gone on for decades, ever since her husband died leaving her a young widow. Praying and fasting, fasting and praying, ignoring priests and prophets, even well-born Pharisees who wagged their heads at her foolishness.

And now . . . well, it was beyond belief. Just like that, they say she flew out of the temple laughing like a lunatic, cornering anyone crazy enough to listen to her babbling about some baby destined to be the Messiah. What in the world had gotten into her?

I find the story of Anna fascinating—three short verses that resonate with joy and intrigue (Luke 2:36–38). Luke tells us little about this woman he calls a prophetess except that she'd been widowed at a young age and had given herself to temple prayer and fasting ever since. One has to wonder if these decades later she just happened to be in the right place at the right time the day Mary and Joseph showed up to have Jesus circumcised. Or is it more likely that she was part of a divine scheme set in motion long before she was born?

Two obscure details in the story seem to indicate that this event was more than mere coincidence. First, Anna was of the tribe of Asher, one of the few who hundreds of years before had returned to Jerusalem to participate in the restoration of Passover at King Hezekiah's request (2 Chronicles 30). That event heralded a time of great revival for people like Anna's ancestors as they braved the scorn of idolatrous Israelites to worship God. Because of her forefathers' zeal for the Lord, Anna's home was Jerusalem, where the Messiah came to call these many generations later.

Second, Anna's father's name was Phanuel, derived from the altar Jacob built after wrestling all night with an angel. It meant *I have seen God face to face, yet my life has been preserved* (Genesis 32:30). Perhaps Anna learned as a young girl at her father's feet of the greatness of their God and the joy of following Him. One can imagine Phanuel explaining his name, telling her stories of a Messiah yet to come, and urging her to seek the face of God with all that was within her.

So what are we to glean from this tiny tidbit of a story that Luke so meticulously records in his history of Christ? I remember reading it for the first time several years ago and being plagued with guilt. I couldn't seem to manage a thirty-minute quiet time and yet this woman did nothing but pray and fast for some sixty-five years. What motivated her? What kept her on her knees when the signs of a Messiah were nowhere in sight? Baffled by her fervor, I longed to learn the secrets of prayer that she possessed.

Then one Sunday morning something happened that gave me a glimpse into Anna's heart. Toward the end of my quiet time as I asked God to do a work that day in our services, a deep cry erupted within me and I began to weep for no apparent reason. Though I did not speak, I knew prayer was pouring forth from my soul. When the tears subsided, I was surprised at the intensity of the experience and overwhelmed with the deep sense of God's presence it brought. For the first time I felt I understood Paul's words that *the Spirit Himself intercedes for us with groanings too deep for words* (Romans 8:26).

The significance of this experience was soon made clear to me while reading a book on fasting.[1] It spoke of the hunger we have for God that can take the form of a deep mourning before Him for His presence in our lives. The key passage was a discussion Jesus had with some of John the Baptist's disciples who were bothered because they fasted but His disciples didn't. Jesus responded cryptically: *The attendants of the bridegroom cannot mourn as long as the bridegroom is with them, can they? But the days will come when the bridegroom is taken away from them, and then they will fast* (Matthew 9:15).

Jesus seemed to be saying that within the heart of His bride, the church, a deep yearning for His presence will reside. Like a young woman whose fiancé has gone away, her heart will ache as she mourns his absence until the day he returns. This is something beyond human experience, for Paul's words imply that the Spirit himself is groaning within us. Why is this? Because the heart-cry of the Godhead is for the presence of Christ to be manifested, captivating souls and raising up worshipers throughout the earth until He is given first place in everything. Indeed, until that final day when He comes in power to establish His awesome reign, the Spirit mourns the loss of the *Bridegroom*'s presence on earth through the prayers of His people.

I believe that though we may not all weep, the Spirit within each of us desires to stir up inimitable longing for more of Jesus. If we open our hearts to this journey in prayer, soon we will find ourselves praying, crying out, pleading for Him to manifest His presence in our hearts, our homes, our cities, our nation, indeed among all the peoples of the earth, so that He might be worthily worshiped. To pray this way is to enter into the very heart of God. These are holy moments.

And like Anna, one day we too may look back upon a life spent in blessed vigils of prayer and fasting. As her heart yearned for the Messiah to come, so too will ours, quickened by the same cry the Holy Spirit continually put within her. Fleeting glimpses of His glorious presence must have driven Anna to her knees over and over again. The fellowship of the Spirit she knew in prayer must have produced a joy she could not resist, even amid tears. This is the treasure at our fingertips as well as we cry out for His coming in Spirit today and in glorious return at the end of time.

Hallelujah, for He came ... and He comes ... and He will come again! This is the prospect that provokes prayer, the cause and consolation for our tears and the expectation that must energize all who are betrothed to Christ, our beautiful *Bridegroom*. With joyful hope we cry out: Yes, Lord, *the Spirit and the bride say, "Come"* (Revelation 22:17).

RESPOND

At salvation we were betrothed to Christ and His Spirit was placed in us as a pledge—much like a young woman receives an engagement ring. We are promised to Him, and our entire life here is to be one of joyful wedding preparation. In what specific ways does your daily life demonstrate that you are preparing for this occasion with joy and expectation?

The most tender and pressing reason we fast and pray and intercede is out of lovesick longing to see Jesus. Our cry as the Bride of Christ joins with the cry of the Holy Spirit, *Come, Lord Jesus.* We want to see our Beloved come—to manifest His reign in our homes, our cities, our nation, our world. How might the spiritual disciplines of fasting and/or prayer change as a result of understanding this?

Ponder your longing for Jesus. Is it growing? Do you delight in Him, crave more of Him, yearn for the day you will see Him face-to-face? Are you learning to persevere by experiencing His presence through the Spirit within you? Reflect on the incomparable wonder of this and write a prayer of response.

A Prayer

O Jesus, how I desire you. You are my beloved, and my heart aches at the thought of you. Your continual kindness only makes me long for more of you. O coming One, how we need your Spirit to make us ready—to provide for you a pure and spotless bride. Blessed Lover of our souls, come to us. Come and reign in our hearts and homes and throughout the earth. Let us see you clearly that we might love you fully. We grieve in your absence; we live in mourning even as we cry out, Maranatha! Come, beloved Bridegroom.

POWER OF GOD

Omnipotent, Sovereign, Unlimited, Boundless, Infinite

REFLECT

Begin today by offering praise to God for who He is. Consider what you know to be true of Him and speak words of exultation. Read 1 Chronicles 29:11–14 phrase by phrase as a prayer, pondering the words and adding your own worship. Spend a few minutes contemplating the power of God, asking the Holy Spirit to illumine your heart to its magnitude.

READ

Read at least two of the following Scriptures and then the devotional: 1 Corinthians 1:18; Romans 1:16; 2 Corinthians 13:4; 2 Peter 1:3; Revelation 5:12.

But we preach Christ crucified, to Jews a stumbling block and to Gentiles foolishness, but to those who are the called . . . Christ the power of God.

1 CORINTHIANS 1:23–24

In the sixth month of the year 1994 a cosmic catastrophe unprecedented in scope ruptured the heavens. Astronomers viewing the event through the newly launched Hubble Space Telescope observed some two dozen pieces of a shattered comet called Shoemaker Levy 9 slamming into the surface of Jupiter. The impact was such that for days debris covering a region larger than Earth remained suspended in Jupiter's clouds.

Physicists contend that if all the nuclear power on planet Earth could be harnessed and released at one time, it would still fall short of the energy explosion that occurred that day when scraps of Shoemaker Levy 9 walloped Jupiter. The largest fragments of the comet were perhaps half a mile in diameter and weighed about a billion tons, one piece alone carrying the force of a million hydrogen bombs going off all at once.

If this seems incomprehensible, consider the sheer enormity of energy at the disposal of *El Shaddai—God the Almighty*. Ponder the staggering idea that the full scope of God's strength, the essence of *dunamis*,[1] broods within the being of Jesus, His Son. What does this mean? What might awaken us to the wonder of this kind of power or send us to our knees before its Source?

The answer Paul would give might surprise us, for he points not to Christ as Creator, Conqueror, or King but to the Cross, where He hung in horrifying disgrace, as the greatest display of supernatural strength (1 Corinthians 1:18). This is foolishness, a mystery beyond our grasp, a paradox we will never understand until we see with spiritual eyes the magnitude of the cosmic catastrophe that put Him there.

When sin invaded this world through Adam and Eve, it was a violent act, an assault against the very holiness of a transcendent God. Shattering the pristine purity of creation, this one decision to disobey the Almighty left nothing the same. So horrid was its effect that God immediately removed His presence from the stench of sin's smoldering remains in the heart of humanity. The very beings God had created to shine forth the beauty of His essence now appeared as rotting carcasses, useless and defiled.

Through one man sin entered into the heart of all, and now we, fallen by our very nature, cannot even begin to grasp the intensity of anger that sin elicits from an infinitely pure God. Though it carries a punishment of death, this is not sufficient to display the extent of His wrath. One man's death, indeed, millions of deaths, would never be enough, so great is God's righteous revulsion.

If we want to see the true catastrophic nature of sin, we must look to a hill called Calvary. Christ crucified was the *power of God* unleashed—unmitigated blasts of holy indignation against sin. With every stripe, in every blow, in the ping of hammer against nail, in each drop of blood and agonizing cry, we see God pouring out upon His Son His wrath against your sin and mine. To vindicate the holiness of His name, God had to employ the full force of His power, exacting through Calvary a punishment that would fit the cosmic crime of the citizens of planet Earth.

Christ crucified was the *power of God* displayed. When the Father laid on Him the iniquity of us all, Jesus felt in every way the full horror of our depravity, the haunting hell of hearts ripped apart by shame. He who knew no sin became sin itself. No human force could have kept the Holy One there to endure such torment; no energy on earth could have held Him in such misery. All the power of His infinite deity was brought to bear in those final moments as the Father stood by while the Son paid a price we may never comprehend, given our humanness.

It is sometimes said by way of comfort that if I were the only one to have sinned, Jesus would still have died, so great is His love. This seems a useless discussion, given the reality that all have sinned. But the truth remains that if I could have been the only one, indeed had I committed only one offense in my entire life, it would still carry infinite weight before the Holy One, demanding punishment proportionate to the deed. So despicable to the heart of a holy God is even the most benign sin that no payment could ever suffice short of His Son's bloody battle on Golgotha. For your sin and for mine, there is only Jesus, the *power of God* unto salvation. To Him be honor and glory forever.

RESPOND

The place where we see the most magnificent display of divine force is on the cross, wherein Christ crucified became the power of God. Do you normally think of the cross as a place of power? What does this mean to you now?

Our redemption is made possible by the power of God that was unleashed to enable Christ to pay the price for our sins. This power enables us to know God, who has called us by His own excellence and glory. Everything we need for life and godliness is thus granted to us. Spend some time pondering the weight of sin that caused a holy God to die such a violent death. Have you seen your own sin as acts of aggression against Him? Why or why not? Contemplate His purity and your iniquity. Write a prayer of response.

A Prayer

Jesus, Power of God, how you turn things upside down. How can I approach you—a King who trades a coronation for crucifixion? I see you hanging there, my Jesus, and am sickened at the shame of my sin. I grieve at the weight you carried to vindicate your righteousness and save me from the wrath I deserve. I remember the day you first exposed the raw depravity of my heart and a primal cry sprang from my innermost being for something mighty enough to set me free. Precious Power of God, your Cross will always remind me of the holiness that demanded such a price. I can never forget or take my salvation lightly. Only let me live worthily of what I have seen, O Crucified One, Power of God.

LION OF THE TRIBE OF JUDAH

Ferocious, Grand, King, Conqueror, Fearful

REFLECT

Be still for a few minutes today, asking God to make His presence real to you. Spend some time honoring Him for all you are learning about His Son. Write down at least three things that you can praise Him for. Worship Him.

READ

Read the following verses slowly and meditatively. Let the image of a great Lion fill your mind as you contemplate what this means about Jesus. After a few minutes of meditation, read the following devotional. Genesis 49:9–10; Revelation 5:4–5; Hosea 11:9–10; Amos 3:8; Joel 3:16.

The Lord roars from Zion . . .
and the heavens and the earth tremble.

JOEL 3:16

The lion is a glorious animal, a symbol throughout history and folklore of power, courage, and nobility. There is something uniquely intriguing about the king of the jungle. A vision of the tawny-toned creature with its magnificent mane, whether sprawling in splendor or stalking in arrogance, can't help but elicit a sense of fear and wonder. Families and nations alike have identified with the beautiful beast, inscribing its likeness on crests and coats of arms and national flags.

In the beloved apostle John's unimaginable vision of eternity some two thousand years ago, his eyes were drawn at one point to a throne. There God Almighty held a scroll that could set in motion the judgments necessary for the culmination of human history and the commencement of the new heaven and earth. John passionately yearned to see the book opened, to discover the secret treasures hidden in its words. When there seemed to be no one worthy to unseal the book, John began to weep. And as he did, a loud voice pierced the air, crying out: *Stop weeping; behold, the Lion that is from the tribe of Judah, the Root of David, has overcome so as to open the book and its seven seals* (Revelation 5:5).

The momentous symbolism behind this lone biblical reference to Jesus as a Lion harks back to the time when Jacob, father of the nation of Israel, called his sons together on his deathbed to bless each one with a prophecy concerning their future. As he came to Judah, he likened him to a young lion that would one day overpower his enemies, earning the adulation and allegiance of all his brothers. Hundreds of years later the prophecy was gloriously fulfilled as the tribe of Judah stormed into battle, carrying a banner etched with the likeness of a lion, to secure the area in the Promised Land for all the other tribes.

When a lion roars in the jungle, he can sometimes be heard up to five miles away in every direction as he marks out territory no other beast dare encroach upon. As a descendent of the tribe of

Judah, Jesus went like a *Lion* to the cross, marking out for himself the territory of our souls. *It is finished!* He roared, discharging a war cry that reverberated through the canyons of eternity, shattering enemy strongholds and establishing once for all the victory of redemption. *He has risen!* the disciples proclaimed, and the echo of that sound fills the hearts of rescued men, reminding us that the land is ours, never again to be taken by enemy forces.

One day the scroll John wept over will surely be unsealed and with it the promise that God's judgments are sure. Jesus, carrying a banner of war, will defend the honor of His name by destroying all that falls short of His glory. Until that remarkable day we live in victory, relishing the joy of overcoming grace. We tremble in His presence, thankful that we who through fear of death were subject to slavery all our lives have seen the evil one rendered powerless by the prowess of our indomitable, conquering King (Hebrews 2:15).

The *Lion of the Tribe of Judah* has roared! Bring on the victory dance, clang the resounding cymbals; death is defeated and God's marvelous reign is established in our hearts. The kingdom has come! His will has been done! Fear no more, for the Lion is worthy to open the scroll! Glorify His name!

RESPOND

The end-time judgments against evil are sealed in God's hands and can be set into motion only because of Christ's victory over darkness through His death and resurrection. In what ways might the reality that God's judgments are sure offer comfort to you in your daily life?

Jesus is a Lion, a warrior who faces for us every skirmish against sin, for He has already won the war and desires to daily empower us with greater freedom in His kingdom. As you look at the day before you, consider all its parts in light of this truth. Thank Him aloud for each situation in which He will demonstrate His power for victories already won.

Jesus, in dying on the cross, engaged in a bloody battle for the territory of your heart. Through His resurrection He has secured the victory, placing the banner for His name in the depths of your soul. Do you live with the wonder and joy of this reality? Why or why not? Ponder this and write a prayer of response.

A Prayer

O glorious King—even now I see you pacing back and forth, ready to roar at every move the evil one makes upon the territory of my heart. You have won it and I am yours; I belong to you. There is safety in the truth that you carry a victory banner always before me in triumph. The reality that you are the Lion of the Tribe of Judah sends a thrill through my soul. I long for you to reveal the weight of such a fact. Let me live in the glorious hope that because you have roared, there are lands to be taken for the sake of your glorious name. In you I hide, in you I rest, in you I find refuge, for you have won it. Hallelujah!

LIGHT OF THE WORLD

Brightness, Dayspring, Sun, Radiance, Luster

REFLECT

Have you ever experienced complete darkness? A place where you literally could not see your hand in front of your face? Spend a few minutes thinking about this (if you haven't experienced it, use your imagination). What can you do when it is that dark? What do you feel?

Now think of the complete darkness that reigns in the hearts and souls of those who've never seen Jesus, the Light of the World. Ponder the darkness from which you've been saved. What did it look like? How did it differ from your life now? How has seeing the Light of Life changed the way you live?

READ

As you read some of the following verses, jot down the things they tell you about Jesus, the *Light of the World*. Ask God to give you a greater understanding of what spiritual darkness is and what you have been given, and why, through the devotional that follows.

1 Timothy 6:15–16; John 1:9; Isaiah 60:1–3; 1 Peter 2:9; Matthew 5:14–16; Revelation 21:23–24.

I am the light of the world.

JOHN 8:12

The kitchen clock tells me it is almost noon, but darkness still grips the horizon. Far away, perhaps, there are brown-baked children basking in the warmth of summer's glow or lovers dazzled by evening vistas of goldenrod pageantry, but for us the sun has not visited at all. Sable skies attend both dawn and dusk, the endless gray of winter binding our spirits like graveclothes.

As missionaries in an Alaskan village, my husband and I learned well of the soul sickness that a sunless existence can inflict. The long winter's darkened days at times produced bleak depression. For me, they were often a chilling reminder that most of our village lived in spiritual darkness as well, ensconced in an eternal night with no hope of escape. To them, and to all who sit in the shadow of death, Jesus declared, *I am the light of the world; he who follows Me shall not walk in the darkness, but shall have the light of life* (John 8:12).

Few realized when Jesus spoke these words that they were reminiscent of the time when darkness hovered over the earth and the infinite Creator called out, *Let there be light*, catapulting a plan almost beyond comprehension into place. In that moment the inestimable essence of Being, the Living God, chose to go public with His glory, to manifest His attributes, His character, and His wondrous ways. Before this, He was clothed in unapproachable light, the joy of His existence known only to himself (1 Timothy 6:16).

When God made us in His image, it was to draw us in, to enable us to actually dwell in His radiant presence. Then our souls, like mirrors, would reflect the splendor of His very self. His eternal plan was to thus fill the earth with His glory, enabling us to live in the endless ecstasy of His light. To this end we were created (Numbers 14:21; Isaiah 43:7).

But all too soon sin reared its ugly head, obscuring the light of God's glory and sentencing humanity to the destructive doom of eternal darkness. Not only was man shut up by it but he also came to love the very conditions that had destroyed him. Could there be a greater tragedy than souls once made for the *Light of the World* being blinded by a web of unending darkness?

Yet our rebellion did not derail God's purpose to fill the earth with His glory. Scripture tells us that even before creation, the Godhead communed over the inevitability of sin and designed a plan that would set apart a people in whom the light of His glory could be restored. We glimpse a shadow of this in Jesus' high-priestly prayer: *Father, I desire that they also, whom Thou hast given Me, be with Me where I am, in order that they may behold My glory* (John 17:24).

This is what Christ purchased with His precious blood on Calvary—a people who would be with Him to see His glory. When He delivers us from sin's dark cell, an amazing thing happens. Our eyes are unveiled to see that which our depravity obscured—that for which we were created and for which we've longed without knowing it. The *Light of the World* shines, and we can't help but become consumed with what we've seen.

Jesus unveiled an even loftier wonder when He proclaimed, *You are the light of the world.* Not only would His children *see* His glory, but now transformed, God-saturated believers would experience the joy of making Him known to those still in darkness. This was the plan set in motion before time began, the way in which God would pursue His passion for a glory-drenched earth. And since the day of Pentecost, Christ's followers have marched forward, glory-bearers bidding others to join in proclaiming *the excellencies of Him who has called us out of darkness into His marvelous light* (1 Peter 2:9).

My happiest times in Alaska were in summer when the sun shone as bright at midnight as it did at noon. Like Rip Van Winkle after his long sleep, the Eskimos came to life all day and most of the night, moving about with joy in the warmth of the summer sun. Fishing, berry-picking, picnicking, partying—our village teemed with vibrant energy. Winter was finally over, and for a few weeks the sun would not set at all.

There is coming a time far more glorious than those sunny reprieves from darkness in our little village. We will have no need of the sun or the moon to shine, for the glory of the Lord will illumine us, and the lamp will be the Lamb who was slain for our sins. Oh, the wonder, the joyful anticipation of that day when we will have the Lord for an everlasting *Light* and our God for our glory ... the days of our mourning will be over (Isaiah 60:20). Come quickly, precious *Light of the World.*

RESPOND

When we meet Him face-to-face in eternity, the brilliance of God's glory will be so bright, there will never be the need for any other source of light. What does this metaphor of light reveal to you about God, His nature, His ways, your life and walk with Him?

God's design is to make us radiant beams of His light, that we might draw people to Him and nations to His glory. Consider the light that now shines in your soul. In what ways is God using you in your home? Your neighborhood? Your work place? What is your heart's cry in this? Write a prayer of response.

A Prayer

Jesus, Light of the World, once I stumbled about in the black of night, oblivious to how terribly I'd lost my way. But then you came with a force stronger than the sun itself, your radiance shattering the darkness and branding me forever with the fire of divine love. O precious Light, why is it that I feel at times more like a flickering candle than a blazing torch? How I cry out for you to shine again—to burn in my heart with a brilliance that consumes all my darkness. Restore my zeal; set me aflame that I might show forth your excellencies to a dying world. If they could see you for even one second, they would fall in adoration, even as I must, O blessed and glorious Light.

HOLY ONE

Hallowed, Sacred, Pure, Sanctified, Consecrated

REFLECT

Quiet your heart and mind before God today. Be still in His presence and hear Jesus speaking to you, saying, *Be holy, as I am holy.* Let these words turn over in your mind several times. What does this mean to you? In stillness, ask God to reveal something of His holiness to your heart. Wait upon Him. Worship Him with a pure heart, yielding freely anything unholy in your heart or life for Him to cleanse and change.

READ

Read a few of the following Scriptures, continuing to maintain a spirit of reverence before the Holy One. Then read the devotional. Mark 1:23–24; Hebrews 12:10; Ephesians 5:25–27; Ephesians 1:3–4; 1 John 2:19–20.

We have believed and have come to know that You are the Holy One of God.

JOHN 6:69

Amid the hype that accompanied the advent of the third millennium, pollsters and pundits evaluated the landscape of American society, seeking to make sense of where we have been and where the coming years might take us as a nation. A study done by Christian researcher George Barna sought to compare the behavior of actively involved Christians with the rest of the culture. His discoveries were sad and sobering. On over sixty lifestyle choices, Barna found few discernible differences between those within and those outside the church.[1]

Though its decline may be gradual—like the frog in the kettle who doesn't know he is slowly dying—a church that resembles the world has *fallen away from the truth*, something Scripture calls apostasy. This seems impossible given the very nature of biblical language concerning God's chosen people. The word for church—*ekklesia*—means those who are *called out*. Believers in Christ are the saints—the consecrated, holy ones. *"Come out from their midst and be separate,"* says the Lord, *"and do not touch what is unclean"* (2 Corinthians 6:17).

The weight of this command springs from God's own essence. He is holy—infinitely pure in all His ways. This is what sets Him apart, making Him completely *other* than anyone or anything. It is not one of God's many attributes, but the fountain of perfection for all of them. So glorious is the reality of His holiness that day and night majestic strains of *Holy, Holy, Holy* can be heard reverberating around His throne as billions of angels sing. Were our hearts to grasp an inkling of this, we might never recover.

Old Testament believers lived with a keen awareness of God's fearsome transcendence. Because they believed His presence rested within the ark of the covenant, they kept it in the inner chamber of the tabernacle, the Holy of Holies. Set completely apart by an impenetrable veil, God's sacred dwelling place was accessible only once a year on the Day of Atonement, when the High Priest offered sacrifices for sins. So hallowed was the area that the priest sprinkled everyone and everything anywhere near the entrance as he came out with the blood from the sacrifice. The fire of the Lord would follow, throwing the people on their faces in reverence and awe.

On one occasion when the priests Nadab and Abihu mixed something God hadn't commanded with their sacrifice, His fire consumed them instantly. Moses, gazing at their dead bodies, solemnly reminded their father, Aaron, of God's warning: *By those who come near Me I will be treated as holy, and before all the people I will be honored* (Leviticus 10:3).

For those of us who live in the light of God's grace, it is difficult to comprehend the weightiness of these things. How comfortably we speak of Jesus' "coming into our heart," not finding ourselves in absolute astonishment that such a thing could happen. We sing of the power of His blood, but do we really believe that without it we would be consumed? And that had He not inaugurated a new and living way through the veil of His broken body, we could never come close to the presence of the *Holy One*?

What Christ has done for His church is a wonder beyond compare. *I will dwell in them and walk among them, and I will be their God, and they shall be My people,* He proclaims, tenderly adding, *and I will welcome you* (2 Corinthians 6:16–17). Can we really imagine what this means? To be welcomed into the presence of God is an awesome thing, requiring a purity we can never achieve, even in our most holy moments.

Could we see afresh the wonder of the Cross, perhaps our hearts might begin to sense how grievous a backslidden church must be to the *Holy One,* who died there. That we trifle with unholy lives in the face of this measure of kindness must be astonishing to the angels who look longingly at the mystery of our redemption. Indeed, an unholy church scorns the precious blood of Jesus, the *Holy One,* who even now stands before the Father pleading our case by the scars on His own body.

Every time we come to God, He receives us anew through the veil of His Son's torn flesh. The amazing grace in this is so compelling that to see it would make clinging to the evil in our culture unthinkable. Seeing our Savior treated with the contempt of unholy lives, especially by those who claim to be His own, would fill our hearts with consuming grief. The promise that He dwells in us and walks among us, even welcomes us as a father, would daily stir our souls to *cleanse ourselves from all defilement of flesh and spirit, perfecting holiness in the fear of God* (2 Corinthians 7:1).

Oh, how we need to recapture something of the awe of our calling and the truth of what it cost the *Holy One*. How glorious to be the church, the called-out ones of God, who through His Son's blood and Spirit's indwelling have the power to be holy, as He is holy. Let us run to Him, pressing through the veil of His suffering, pleading for Him to sanctify our hearts and transform our lives that His name might be hallowed once again.

RESPOND

God is holy, a reality that terrifies demons and causes His people to bow in awe, pursuing with zeal lives that honor Him, once they see it. Since Jesus shed His own blood that we might enter the Holy of Holies without being utterly destroyed, what do you think an unholy church means to Him? What areas of unholiness might there be in your own life that you have taken lightly or at least have not realized their impact?

God has chosen to prove himself holy by purifying a people to follow hard after Him that they might actually share in His holiness and demonstrate His worth to the world in response. God's holiness is a glorious thing. Do you find yourself in awe that He has invited you to partake of it, that He actually welcomes you into the fearful place of His incomparable splendor? Ask God to write the truth of His holiness on your heart and make it known in your spirit. Write a prayer in response.

A Prayer

O my Lord, my heart is overwhelmed. I cannot for a minute take lightly the mystery that you welcome me, that within the veil of your awesome holiness, you have made a place for my soul to dwell. How unholy my heart is to ever turn to lesser things. How I grieve before you even now, my Lord, and plead once again the blood of Christ to cover me, cleanse me, sweep me into your presence until my life resonates with the purity of your beauty. Truly I am at your mercy, and in this I find comfort and hope, my Jesus, Holy One.

SERVANT

Helper, Aide, Supporter, Attendant

REFLECT

Read Psalm 116:1–2 as a prayer to the Lord, welcoming Him to this time with you. Thank Him for these truths, offering a heart of love, expressing words of adoration. Contemplate for a few minutes all the benefits that are yours through Christ—cleansing from sin, new life, steadfast love, fresh mercy every morning, strength for each day—make your own list. Look at verses 12 and 13 of this chapter of Psalms. David wondered how He could ever repay God for all that he'd been given. What was his answer in verse 13? What do you think this means? Why do you think it glorifies God for us to raise the cup of salvation, always asking for more?

As you come to learn of Him, hold your own cup up to Jesus—empty, dirty, fragile, or broken though it may be. Let Him take it to cleanse, restore, and bring salvation to your soul once again through your time with Him.

READ

Read at least two of the following verses and then the devotional: Matthew 12:18; Isaiah 53:11; Isaiah 49:6; Acts 17:24–25; Romans 15:8–11.

> *For even the Son of Man did not come to be served,*
> *but to serve, and to give His life a ransom for many.*
>
> MARK 10:45

I saw it again the other day—another televangelist garbed in Armani, sporting diamonds, and extolling the blessings of belonging to Christ. To the casual observer, these kinds of claims must seem too good to be true—a god who serves people like a genie brought forth from a bottle by faith. Is this what Jesus meant when He said He came not to be served but to serve? And if this isn't the way He serves us, then what is? Perhaps even more important: Why would the infinite God, perfect in all His ways and in need of nothing, lower himself to serve humanity?

Trying to grasp Jesus' role as *Servant* within the context of His exaltation is not easy. How do we reconcile His radiant beauty with a face marred by the spittle of man? How do we juxtapose His status as Supreme upon the lowly vagabond who rode into town on a donkey? And how can we possibly integrate the Godhead's glorious power with the battered convict who fell on his face, unable even to carry His own cross?

This was the struggle Peter faced as Jesus knelt to wash the disciples' feet in His final hours. The brash fisherman recoiled at the notion of his Master serving him in such a menial manner, insisting this could never be. But Scripture tells us that Jesus did this *knowing that the Father had given all things into His hands, and that He had come forth from God, and was going back to God* (John 13:3). There is a wondrous mystery here, for when Jesus took up the towel and girded himself to serve, not only was He fully aware of His power, glory, and divine nature, but He chose to wash their feet precisely because of it.

This was because He wanted to write a message on their hearts and ours, to paint a picture that could never be forgotten concerning His relationship with fallen creatures. In short, Jesus set out to demonstrate that the Son of Man came not to be served but to serve, for we would always be in need of Him, not the other way around. In serving humanity, the glory of His power to save would beam brightly against the canopy of our sin.

This was driven home for me one day recently as I performed a pedicure for a crippled, homeless woman. Though I tried to elicit conversation while massaging her feet in the warm water, she continually looked the other way, clearly embarrassed by the situation. As I prayed silently over the suffering that permeated her life, I began to sense why this was so difficult for her. For her to place herself in such a position before me only magnified my strength and health, making her more painfully aware of her own condition.

In the same way, when Jesus came to us as a *Servant,* the filth of our fallen flesh served to magnify the beauty of His perfection, making it clear that we are always the ones in desperate need. *If I do not wash you, you have no part with Me,* He told Peter, reminding us that without the cleansing of His blood, we could not come to Him at all.

To have *a part* in Jesus requires that He serve us, for we simply have nothing to bring to the table. He serves us at salvation by cleansing us from our sins and then throughout our life by filling us with His Spirit. He pours out His gifts upon us that we might serve others, becoming stewards of His manifold grace. Peter reminds us that we are always dependent upon God, even in our most zealous moments. *Whoever speaks,* he writes, *let him speak, as it were, the utterances of God. Whoever serves,* he emphasizes, *let him do so as by the strength which God supplies.* Day by day, moment by moment, Jesus comes to wash our feet by giving us abundant grace *so that in all things God may be glorified through Jesus Christ, to whom belongs the glory and dominion forever and ever. Amen* (1 Peter 4:11).

This makes it very clear that in serving us, Jesus is actually serving himself and His glorious cause to raise up worshipers from every tongue and tribe. It isn't enough, God said long ago, for my *Servant* to save the Jews only. I will make Him *a light of the nations so that My salvation may reach to the end of the earth* (Isaiah 49:6). When Jesus gave himself as a ransom for many, it was so that the multiplied magnificence of His saving power might shine like a million points of light across this globe and back to the heart of the Father, filling Him with pleasure.

The glory of God through the salvation of souls is Jesus' ultimate purpose in serving humankind. This is why, though fully God, He became fully man, a bondservant to the point of death on a cross. This too is why the Father has now highly exalted Him and given Him the name before which one day every knee will bow and proclaim His Lordship *to the glory of God the Father* (Philippians 2:6–11). Let us fall before our *Servant King* and receive from Him once again that we might glorify His name forever.

RESPOND

Jesus came as a Servant for His Father's glory and the exaltation of His name. Scripture teaches that Jesus serves us by granting us salvation and giving us grace, the divine enabling we need to do all the works that will bring Him exaltation. When we rely on grace for the acts of service we bring, we will find ourselves laboring with joy and zeal. Is this your experience? Why or why not?

God does not need us, for He made the world and everything in it. As His creation, we have nothing to bring to Him but empty, needy hearts. If we serve Him because we believe He needs us or is somehow enhanced by our labor, we dishonor Him. Ponder this and write a prayer of response.

A Prayer

Jesus, how can I ever offer anything to you who created the world and everything in it? How could I think that you might be served by these hands of flesh? Yet you choose to use me for your glory and grant me everything I need for such a thing. I am humbled, O Lord, and overwhelmed at what you offer. Awaken me to the truth that you have no hunger I can fill, no need I can abate. Make me a helpless, empty-handed beggar once again. Come and wash my feet today that I might serve you and, in serving, glorify your name, O precious Servant.

THE TRUTH

Substance, Veracity, Integrity, Reality, Fact

REFLECT

Wait in stillness for a few minutes before God today. Settle your soul, resting in the reality of His presence, asking Him to enable you to hear His voice. Hear Jesus speaking to you, *I am the Truth.* Consider situations you are facing right now that are difficult, confusing, and uncertain. Hear Him again, saying, *I am the Truth.* What does this mean to you?

READ

Prayerfully seek illumination as you read the following Scriptures and the devotional: John 14:6; Romans 1:18–19; Romans 1:25; 1 John 5:20.

Jesus said to him, "I am . . . the truth."

JOHN 14:6

What is truth? Pilate jabbed at Jesus in the final moments before turning Him over to His executioners. Then, as if regretting having asked, the procurator of Judea walked out and washed his hands, absolving himself forever of his failure to find the answer.

What *is* truth? Leo Tolstoy, Russia's premier writer of the nine-teenth century, found himself tormented by this question during what should have been his happiest years. Having produced two literary masterpieces, he was highly regarded for his intellect by all strata of society. He loved his wife, adored his children, and enjoyed great wealth. Yet looking across the landscape of his life, he saw only a series of incoherent and pointless images. Though the world and its treasures were at his fingertips, suicidal depression consumed him.

"The truth is that life is meaningless," Tolstoy finally concluded. In his autobiography written much later, he details how he came to this place of quiet despair even at the height of worldly success.[1] It began with bursts of bewilderment in his quiet moments. The ques-tions "Why?" and "What next?" baffled him, tormenting his mind with a demand for answers. Slowly these spurts of painful analysis grew, melding together until he was incapable of a moment's peace. The misery of meaninglessness haunted him at every point.

One night he engaged in a series of mental exercises, question-ing all aspects of his life. When he came to his fame, he mused, "Very well, you will be more famous than Gogol, Pushkin, Shake-speare, Moliere, more famous than all the writers in the world—so what?" To his utter dismay, Tolstoy discovered that he could find absolutely no reply.

From there the literary genius entered a season of terror. Fear-ing he might take his own life, he removed a rope from his room at night and gave up his gun when traveling. He writes that he was as "a man lost in the forest who was terrified by the fact that he was lost." Oddly enough, this desperation kept Tolstoy alive. He was baffled by his need for answers and began to believe that his very compulsion to ask why was evidence that an answer existed, for if life held no meaning, then surely he would not care so very much.

When Jesus claimed to be the *Truth*, He answered the "why" and "what next" of every person. In this simple declaration, He reminds us that because we are created in the image of God, the knowledge that something transcends us is written on the fabric of our souls. To be human is to have an awareness, a sense of "otherness" churning within, forcing us to ask the questions that can lead us back to our Creator to find the real meaning of our lives.

Of course, sin-sick people forever engage in pointless pursuits that deny this reality. Instead of seeking the One for whom we were created, we construct elaborate schemes to justify our rejection of God. Perhaps, like Pilate, to accept the reality of His existence would demand a response we can't afford to give. Thus we suppress the truth, ascribing meaning to such minutiae as the houses we live in or the lovers we embrace, the children we bear or the successes we achieve. All the while the flicker of hope in our hollowed-out hearts slowly extinguishes. To this universally desolate condition Jesus proclaimed, *I am the Truth*, tenderly extending a way out of the forest of emptiness and back to the Father himself.

Tolstoy wrote of the epiphany that saved his life in the midst of his darkest days. Reassessing the Christian faith of his childhood, he told of how he realized that if he had not lived with a vague hope of finding God, he would have killed himself long before. Thus he decided the meaning of life must be rooted in the existence of God. He writes, " 'What, then, do I seek?' a voice cried out within me. 'He is there, the one without whom there could be no life.' "

Yes, He is there—*in Him we live and move and exist* (Acts 17:28). Jesus is the spiritual center, the source of everything real. Without Him all we might cling to is a lie, every purpose we embrace only vanity. And when He comes to us as the *Truth*, Jesus offers no less than the unfolding of himself and a chance to participate in His eternal plan, to at last pursue the purpose for which we were born. When we grasp this and fall at His feet in worship, surrendering our life into His hands, we will know that *The Truth* has come and set us free.

RESPOND

There is one objective reality that lies at the base of all existence—the living God who has always been and always will be. Jesus the Truth is the manifestation of that reality to us. Consider your personal awareness of a transcendent God. When did you first sense it? What questions led you to Jesus the Truth?

Within the heart of every person is the knowledge of the objective reality called God, for He has put it there. We spend our life suppressing this reality, believing this world offers more pleasure than the God who made us. Does your daily purpose for living find focus in Jesus the Truth? How does your life demonstrate that He is the *center* of your existence, the delight of your days?

Not only are we granted the privilege of knowing Him who is true, but we are *in* Him who is true. What does this mean to you? Write a prayer of response.

A Prayer

O Jesus, how empty my striving for answers was until I found you. I am in awe, profoundly grateful, and yet I grieve. Many around me still suppress your truth in unrighteousness, and I cannot help but mourn. Even your own children seem lost at times, groping for solutions like needles in the haystack of this world's greedy gods. How desperately we need you to come, O Truth that cannot be denied, and startle us from the reverie that rejection of you has wrought. Expose the empty answers and vacuous charms of the idols of this age. Awaken worshipers from every corner of the globe to find their hope in you and lay down their lives in worship. Be the Center, my Lord, for from you and through you and to you are all things, Jesus, wondrous Truth.

THE WORD

Message, Utterance, Declaration,
Expression, Voice, Revelation

REFLECT

Is your vision of the exalted Christ expanding? In what ways? Spend a few minutes thinking of Jesus as He is normally viewed by the people you know, even other believers. Now consider some of the things you are learning. Look back over your prayer journal and begin to praise Him for fresh facets of His glory. Bow your heart, or maybe even your knees, before Him today, asking Him to impress you with the reality of His glorious Being.

READ

Read the Scriptures that follow and then the devotional: John 1:1–2, 14; 1 John 1:1–2; Hebrews 1:1–2; Luke 24:27.

His name is called The Word of God.

REVELATION 19:13

His name was Patrick, and he stepped ashore in Dane, Ireland, in A.D. 433 as a newly ordained priest, burning with passion to spread the gospel of Jesus Christ. The young man could not have known that day that he was about to begin a ministry that would alter the course of Christian history.

This wasn't his first trip to Ireland. Years before he'd been abducted from his home in Britain and made a slave by Irish warlords who assigned him the job of sheepherder. For hours on end he had roamed the rolling, verdant hills, and like the shepherd boy David thousands of years before, Patrick came to know God intimately, seeking His face in prayer day in and day out.

One night after six years in captivity Patrick heard God speak, telling him he would be going home, for a ship some two hundred miles away was ready to take him. Patrick writes that though he'd never been to the shore and knew no one there, he simply packed up and fled in the middle of the night. With God's guidance and strength, he eventually found the ocean, where through a series of miracles he did indeed gain passage on a ship.

When he made it back to Britain at last, Patrick discovered that much of the great Roman Empire, of which his homeland had been a part, had crumbled as a result of wave after wave of barbarian attack. Burning and looting with reckless abandon, they had destroyed entire cities, leaving little intact. Feeling lost and abandoned, Patrick finally found a family to take him in, but soon he began having a series of dreams in which a man stood before him, holding many letters. He writes,

> And he gave me one of them, and I read the opening words of the letter, which were *The voice of the Irish*; and as I read the beginning of the letter I thought that at the same moment I heard their voice . . . and thus did they cry out as with one mouth: "We ask thee, boy, come and walk among us once more." And I was quite broken in heart, and could read no further, and so I woke up . . .
>
> And another night—whether within me or beside me, I

know not, God knoweth—they called me most unmistakably
with words which I heard but could not understand, except
that at the end of the prayer He spoke thus: "He that has laid
down His life for thee, it is He that speaketh in thee"; and so
I awoke full of joy.[1]

Patrick knew beyond any doubt that God was calling him back
to Ireland to bring them the gospel of Jesus Christ. Immediately he
pursued the training he needed to become a priest and found himself at last on Ireland's shores once again. This would be the beginning of some forty years of faithful ministry, seeing God continually
work in miraculous ways.

Saint Patrick (as we know him today) worked tirelessly, wit-
nessing the conversion of thousands of pagans. When he died, Ireland was almost completely evangelized. He left behind a heritage
of multiple monasteries, housing hundreds of monks who learned
to read and write by copying all the classical literature of Rome,
including the Old and New Testaments.

Hundreds of years later historians began to see the vast significance of Patrick's ministry. During his time in Ireland, massive raids
on the Roman Empire destroyed all the great libraries of Western
Europe. From a human standpoint, this might have been the end
of the Bible, the finale to the written Word of God. But in the
quietness of countryside monasteries, God preserved His precious
Logos through the elementary education of once barbarian monks
who now lived for His cause.

The story of Saint Patrick is only one glorious thread in a tapestry woven throughout history, demonstrating God's esteem for
the sacred Scriptures that now adorn bookshelves and pews and
coffee tables throughout our land. Why such zeal? For what purpose such fervor? All God has ever done to preserve the value of
His written Word has sprung from a passion to display and uphold

His Son, the living *Word*. Jesus is the One to whom all Scripture points and for whom every iota of God-breathed Scripture exists. *"You search the Scriptures because you think that in them you have eternal life,"* He admonished the Pharisees, *"and it is these that bear witness of Me"* (John 5:39).

Jesus, the living *Word*, was with God and *was* God. This God, who once spoke worlds into being, spoke His very essence into the womb of a woman that we might finally know Him as He is. Jesus is the glorious and ultimate manifestation of a God who delights to disclose himself to us. This is why the *Word* incarnate causes the written Word to teem with precious life.

Let us come faithfully to the Scriptures, anticipating daily the miracle of encounter with the *Word*, whose very Being pulses from each page. Let us cherish every letter, jot, and tittle of the written Word, seeking always to find in them the face of Jesus, the *Word* who lives and breathes and transforms us by His every touch. O sacred *Word*, blessed *Word*, Living *Word*, Jesus.

RESPOND

All Scripture is God-breathed, holy and precious, for it points the way to the Word Incarnate, Jesus. This was the truth He emphasized over and over to His disciples and one that they preached continually in the early church. What value do you place on Scripture? What is your goal when you read, study, meditate, or memorize it? Do you come to it regularly, seeing it as a treasure, opening the way to an encounter with Jesus?

In the Word, who became flesh, we find eternal life. Because He came and dwelt among us, suffering in our place, we can one day walk in glory, delighting in the fullness of His glory. Jesus is the very Word of God, life-breathing, energizing, transforming Word. Meditate on this and write a response.

A Prayer

Jesus, Word of God, from glory you came and spoke with your life—feeding the hungry, teaching the masses, befriending sinners, healing the broken, touching the wounded, chastising the proud, embracing the weak . . . dying on Calvary. You spoke, O Word, and then to glory you returned. I rejoice for I have beheld your glory, but oh, how I ache for more. I need your presence to permeate the dullness that plagues my heart. I am divided and distracted—the sound of your voice at times a distant memory. So I cry out for you to come, to speak once again with the two-edged sword that will pierce me to my core, reminding me once again of the beauty that you, O Word, became flesh and dwelt among us.

STUMBLING BLOCK

Offense, Scandal, Affront, Snare, Hindrance

REFLECT

As you come before the Lord today, spend a few minutes speaking aloud His attributes and praising Him for them (for a list, see Psalm 145). Enter His courts with thanksgiving and praise as you let worldly distractions fade away. Honor Him with words of worship.

Consider for a moment times when you have had (or even are now having) difficulty trusting God with the direction of your life. Have you taken offense at Him? Become bitter? Resisted His will? What do you do when His ways don't make sense to you? Ask the Holy Spirit to reveal truth to you concerning these things today.

READ:

Read the following Scriptures: 1 Corinthians 1:22–23; 1 Peter 2:6–8; Lamentations 3:37–40; and the following devotional.

---

*Behold, I lay in Zion a stone of stumbling and a
rock of offense, and he who believes in Him
will not be disappointed.*

ROMANS 9:33

It was a miracle that catapulted Christ into fame, having filled its observers with holy fear and a sense that God had indeed come. On an otherwise ordinary day, Jesus and a large crowd of followers encountered a massive funeral procession outside a small town called Nain. Gazing at the widow who'd lost her only son, Jesus tenderly uttered, *Stop weeping.* Then touching the coffin's side, He called out, *Young man, I say to you, arise!* To the astonishment of all, the dead man sat up and began talking, even as Jesus handed him over to his stunned mother. Scripture says the report of this resurrection went out all over Judea and the surrounding district.

When John the Baptist, who languished in a dark prison cell, heard the news, he appealed to two of his followers to go and investigate. Soon they caught up with Jesus, asking as John had instructed them, *Are you the expected one, or shall we look for someone else?*

In response, Jesus performed a host of miracles before their very eyes and then exhorted them: *"Go and report to John what you have seen and heard: the blind receive sight, the lame walk, the lepers are cleansed, and the deaf hear, the dead are raised up, the poor have the gospel preached to them."* Then in what almost seemed an afterthought, Jesus added, *"God blesses those who are not offended by me"* (Luke 7:22–23 NLT).

Why John sent these men at this time is a mystery. Maybe he simply wanted Jesus to know his fate. Perhaps he needed some words of encouragement or the reassurance that Jesus was indeed the One worth dying for. Whatever the reasons, Jesus' unusual answer established something with which every serious seeker must come to terms—that to follow Him means to grapple with the offensive, illogical ways of a God who won't be hijacked by human reasoning no matter how religious its overtones.

The Greek word for *offense* is *skandalizo,* from which we derive our word *scandalous.*[1] Jesus often says and does scandalous things that upend our arrogant assessments of how a good God should behave. He shuns the religious elite to dine with prostitutes and drunkards and thieves. He offers the faithful servant who has spent a lifetime in ministry the same wage as a murderer who makes a deathbed profession of faith. He balks at pompous piety and pours out grace on the needy. He turns sons against mothers and allows His most faithful followers to be martyred, ever demolishing the sanctuary of our "God boxes."

There will be times for each of us when to follow this Jesus will mean having our safety nets pulled out from under us. Our creeds may no longer comfort, and questions may come from the very dogma we once defended, as we learn firsthand that like Aslan in *The Chronicles of Narnia,* though Jesus is good, He is certainly not safe. For John this meant being shut up in prison, his life about to end in a gruesome way even though he'd spent it faithfully heralding the coming of Christ. We can almost imagine Jesus' tender admonition to the cousin He so loved: *Don't be offended at this, John—your very happiness rests in not stumbling over that which you cannot understand.*

In the end, to follow this Jesus is to come to the place where we cease to stumble over Him, though there may be moments of conflict and seasons of darkness. Once He has secured our devotion with His everlasting love, we will continually choose to give up our rights, our wisdom, and our control, indeed our very lives, for from the core of our soul we know that He is worthy. In those times of despair, in those still and quiet moments when we cannot see His face, we may hear Him gently whisper, *"You do not want to go away also, do you?"* But like Peter, we will have no other answer than *Lord, to whom shall we go? You have the words of eternal life* (John 6:68).

In this we affirm forever that nothing is lovelier than our Lord, that He is joy, even as we partake in the fellowship of His suffering. Truly, when we know this Jesus, we delight to humbly bow and put our trust in Him, for our happiness depends on it.

RESPOND

To follow Jesus is to walk a path that will often not make sense to the natural mind. As a *stumbling block,* He will call us to works or decisions that fly in the face of this world's values. Are there any areas of your life currently that demonstrate this reality?

To walk with Jesus is to wrestle at times with His words, His plans, and His ways and yet to find the joy in not being offended at what He is doing or has done. Have you discovered this *happiness* that Jesus speaks of, that comes from not stumbling over His ways? How might the way you handle difficulty demonstrate the worth of your Lord?

The joy of faith comes in knowing Him as He is—the One who has eternal life in His hands and who alone is holy—perfect in all His ways: in justice, righteousness, goodness, mercy, peace. Ponder this and write a prayer of response.

A Prayer

Jesus, how often I have stumbled, raising my foolish hands in rebellion at what I cannot explain. And yet you so patiently draw me back to you, to the place where I remember your worth—your glorious, wonderful worth—and I can only wor-ship you once again. How vain to be offended at you, O great God of the Universe, who holds the worlds together by your power. Teach me, Lord, to honor you by trusting even when my flesh is afraid and my carnal mind seeks relief. You alone are holy, in you alone are the words of eternal life—to whom else could I ever go, my Jesus, for you have become the Rock of my salvation.

THE HEAD

Source, Chief, Commander, Highest,
All in All, First and Last

REFLECT

As you come to Jesus today, do you see Him as all-sufficient? The fountain from which you may always drink? Do you approach prayer as a taking in, an imbibing of the wonderful nectar of His presence? Or do you see it as something you do, something you achieve, or as a way in which you impress or assist God?

Spend a few minutes today acknowledging from within that you are the receiver and God is the Giver. Bring your weakness, your lack of discipline, your selfish agendas, and offer them to Him that they might be transformed into His workmanship for His glory. Rest in the reality that He is all in all.

READ

Read prayerfully a few of the following Scriptures, asking God to give you His heart for the church and Christ's role in it. When He has spoken, read the devotional. Ephesians 4:15–16; 1 Corinthians 12:27; Ephesians 1:22–23; Romans 15:5–7.

> *He is also head of the body, the church . . . so that*
> *He Himself might come to have first place in*
> *everything.*
>
> COLOSSIANS 1:18

Rwanda in April 1994! Who can forget the terrible scenes of thousands of corpses floating down the Akagera River to Lake Victoria? An eyewitness wrote, "First came the corpses of the men and elder boys, killed trying to defend their sisters and mothers. Then came the women and girls, flushed out from their hiding places and slaughtered. Last came the babies."[1]

In the now famous genocide perpetuated by the Hutu tribe against the minority Tutsis in the tiny nation of Rwanda, almost a million people were murdered within a few days as millions more fled into exile. Perhaps the most grievous aspect of this nightmare was that 80 to 90 percent of the Rwandan people considered themselves Christian at the time. The famous East African revival of the 1930s had deeply evangelized the country, having seen over one thousand people baptized per week during its peak.

In the years following this horrible human slaughter Christian leaders from the Vatican in Rome to mission boards in America agonized, tormented by the question "Where was the church?" Some speculated that the revival had been too hyper-spiritual, failing to impact the real living of life and socio-political structure in the ethnically hostile country. Some accused the church leaders of having sold their souls to the government, rendering impotent the prophetic voice that was so desperately needed when the killing began. Still others blame the missionaries, who taught Christian love but demonstrated divisiveness—Lutheran and Baptist, Catholic and Presbyterian, Seventh-Day Adventist and Methodist—that in the end subtly lent credence to the abhorrent antagonism between Hutus and Tutsis. Most disturbing of all were allegations that leaders in the church actually encouraged and participated in the mass murders.

Whatever the truth may be, the church became almost invisible amid the killing fields of the Rwandan genocide. Such a shameful indictment should have tolled its death knell. Yet, in fact, after the war it was the church that began building orphanages for the fatherless children and helping broken widows put the pieces of their lives back together. Today, some seven years later, many churches there are quietly facilitating restoration and reconciliation. A group of Canadian Christians who recently traveled to Rwanda writes the following account of a service they attended:

> Catholic priests and Protestant pastors standing with thousands in a football stadium, praying as one in the name of Jesus ... Hutu young people weeping uncontrollably on the shoulders of their Tutsi peers ... widows dancing and weeping for joy in the very place where their husbands and children were hacked to death; thousands of street orphans surging forward at the assurance that God their Father really does love them and He does cartwheels of delight for joy of their company.[2]

With a history of extraordinary starts and startling stops, of glorious rises and disgraceful descents, the church of Jesus Christ somehow marches on. Even amid its darkest days, a force that far transcends Satan's schemes or the horror of humankind's sin has always been at work, guaranteeing that the church will not die.

Since the outpouring of His Spirit at Pentecost, Jesus has personally baptized every newly saved soul into a living organism He calls His body. As the *Head*, He is the instrument of life through which this body is built up in love. Jesus supplies all that His body needs—strength for the weakest member and grace for every defect of our fallen condition. He loves the church as He loves His very self, nourishing, cherishing, and caring for it with tender affection (see Ephesians 6).

In some mysterious way, the Father has condescended to more magnificently glorify His Son through us with all our flaws than without us. When we consider Jesus' infinite supremacy, how can we ever fathom "this highest honor of the church, that the Son of God regards himself as in a certain sense imperfect unless he is joined to us."[3] This reality should arrest our hearts, consuming us with zeal for our Father's house.

The church—in Rwanda, Germany, China, Saudi Arabia, Russia, India, America, Turkmenistan, Lithuania, Bangladesh, Afghanistan, Mauritius, and throughout the world—will ever stand. It is protected not by the work of human hands, or the strength of its members, or by the commitment of missionaries, but by Jesus Christ, the *Head* of the body, who fills all in all. In whatever desperate straits it may at times find itself, the church of Jesus Christ cannot fail, for its *Head* sits at the right hand of God, determined to bring about a day when He will have first place in everything (Colossians 1:18).

This mystical organism called Christ's body cannot help but advance with supernatural energy, for it is the means by which He has chosen to build His kingdom. Wonder of wonders that our destiny as His body is to be the radiant and visible manifestation of Christ's fullness on earth. Perhaps we see it only now as in a glass darkly, but one day the church will reign triumphant with the full and magnificent splendor worthy of Jesus Christ, our *Head*. What a day of glory that will, at last, be.

RESPOND

Jesus is the Head of the body, the church, a living organism created to manifest the fullness of His glorious being. Pause and consider the extreme implausibility of such a thing. Is this how you view the church? If not, why? How does your commitment to it compare to the value Christ places on the church, His body?

Jesus even now is supplying all that we need for the church to become a glorious vision of His greatness. What do you think hinders this in your own life? Your church? The church at large?

Everything God does in our lives, in the church and in the world, has one goal—that Jesus be given first place in everything. This is the foundation of every prayer we pray—that Christ might be the Head—prevailing in power and authority in every situation. Ponder this and write a prayer of response.

A Prayer

Dearest Lord, how simple and wonderful is this plan for your dignity and authority to be manifest here through us, your body. Yet it seems we settle for lesser goals. We strive for success, fight for fulfillment, wrestle for rights, and pursue personal preeminence. How did we lose our way? When did we abandon our connection to you, our only Head? One glance at your church confronts us with the gravity of such a thing—a body with no head cannot survive. O God, open our eyes to the glory of a church where you, our Head, reign and everything flows from the beauty of your supremacy. Come and rule once again—in our lives, our homes, your church, our world—come in power, come in authority, for we have no other hope but that you reign, O glorious Head.

KING OF KINGS

Uncontested Ruler, Ultimate Authority,
Everlasting Government, Ineffable Majesty

REFLECT

Read Psalm 145:10–16 slowly out loud as praise to God. Ponder the words in verse 13, prayerfully meditating on their meaning. What is God showing you? What does His dominion tell you about Jesus himself? Wait in God's presence, asking Him to reveal himself to you today.

READ

Read at least two of the following verses and then the devotional: 1 Timothy 6:13–16; Revelation 4:2; Daniel 2:44; Isaiah 40:23; Psalm 102:15.

And on His robe and on His thigh He has a name
written, "King of Kings."

REVELATION 19:16

Majestic strains of Handel's *Messiah* wafted into the air for the first time in the year 1742 from a music hall in Dublin, Ireland.

Since that day appreciation for the masterpiece has flourished throughout the world, making it one of the most central and delightful components in celebrating the birth of Christ. The miracle of the music is perhaps surpassed only by the extraordinary way in which George Frederic Handel composed it.

Handel was at a crossroads at that time, his future prospects grim. After having enjoyed two decades of popularity, his life had taken a desolate twist. He lost his fortune, was abandoned by many friends, censored by the church, and partially paralyzed by a stroke.

One wintry morning Handel shut himself in his studio and for the next twenty-four days focused on writing music, rarely stopping to eat or drink. Toward the end of his self-imposed exile, a servant entered Handel's studio to find him with tears streaming down his face. Looking up, Handel exclaimed, "I think I did see all heaven before me, and the great God himself!" The time spent behind closed doors composing had been an epiphany for the forlorn musician. The result was the *Messiah*.

I have loved Handel's *Messiah* since the first time I sang it in high school chorus. I've listened to it scores of times, and the depths of truth and heights of hope so passionately reflected in the music and lyrics never fail to stir me. Like King George II, who flew to his feet at the first strains of the "Hallelujah Chorus," every time I hear those familiar words—"King of Kings and Lord of Lords"— my heart takes flight.

The reality that Jesus is *King of Kings* is the greatest news the gospel has to offer. Christ reigns—times and seasons and our hearts as well are in His hands. The Sovereign Son to whom all authority has been given does not stand in heaven shuddering at the horrors of humanity or wringing His hands, hoping mere mortals will come to His aid. His dominion *rules over all* (Psalm 103:19).

Yes, there is a King—He is the *King of Kings,* whose rule is eternal. Civilizations rise in power and glory only to be reduced to paragraphs in history books, but the government that rests on Christ's shoulders will never end. His reign is absolute, unlimited, and independent of any other person or thing. He has never needed a coronation, for His Kingship is intrinsic to His very existence.

There *is* a kingdom, and the *King of Kings* reminds us that though it is not of this world, His reign is as real as the very air we breathe. It is a glorious kingdom, for the King is exquisite in His manifold perfections. His rule is one of perfect justice, punctuated by endless love and imposed through infinite power.

Those of us blessed to be subjects of this kingdom serve willingly, for the reign of our Monarch resounds with wonder and delight. We live with longing to see the fruition of His rule in our hearts, our homes, our cities, our nation, and throughout the world. *Thy kingdom come* resonates with every prayer we pray.

Jesus is *King of Kings,* a joy that rings from our depths in faith-filled worship. He is a worthy King, deserving full allegiance and lives that bear testimony to the splendor of His ways. When once we've walked in the presence of His majesty, our souls find purpose only in bowing before Him in loyalty and submission. For every soul into whose heart He has come to reign, there is a future and a hope, even in the face of life's greatest trials. The profound truth that the kingdoms of this world will one day become the kingdom of our Lord and of His Christ takes us to the heights of lofty praise as it did so long ago in the heart of George Frederic Handel (Revelation 11:15).

> *King of Kings, and Lord of Lords,*
> *King of Kings and Lord of Lords.*
> *And He shall reign forever and ever.*
> *Forever and ever, forever and ever.*
> *Hallelujah! Hallelujah! Hallelujah!*
> *Hallelujah! Hallelujah!*

RESPOND

There is one eternal fact that gives perspective and meaning to every other reality: "Behold, a throne . . ." How would a continual realization of this affect the daily details of your life? What situations are you facing that gain an entirely different perspective in light of Christ's eternal reign?

Handel "saw" something that day in his studio. Paul would say he was given a spirit of wisdom and revelation in the knowledge of God, that his eyes were enlightened to the hope of his calling (Ephesians 1:17–18). Has this been your experience? Have you had a time or times when your spirit was awakened to the wonder and incredible beauty of Jesus, *King of Kings*? If not, begin making these words your heart-cry today and in the coming days as you come before Him: "Jesus, show me your majesty."

The reign of Jesus as *King of Kings* is a glorious one. His majesty and splendor are beyond description. When we glimpse the *King of Kings* on His throne, we are stunned by His beauty, humbled at our inadequacy, and compelled to speak of what we have seen. Ponder the throne of the *King of Kings*. Look into the face of the One who rules over all. Worship Him. Write a prayer of response.

A Prayer

Jesus, King of Kings, I am yearning for the day your kingdom comes in power, for even momentary impressions of your dominion leave me breathless. I am astounded by the magnificence of your majesty and in awe of your sovereign splendor. I worship you, worthy King. My mouth cannot keep silent—I must tell of your mighty acts and make known the glory of your kingdom. Daily, my King, I sense the dissatisfaction of living in a fallen world, where evil resonates from the thrones of men. We need your reign—nothing else will do. Come, O King of Kings, and rule, dissolving all other dominions beneath your feet. Magnify your name until every knee yields under the weight of your glory.

CONSUMING FIRE

Arduous Inferno, Unquenchable Flame,
Uncontainable Blaze, Holy Holocaust

REFLECT

Fire ... what comes to your mind at this word? Why do you think Scripture uses this metaphor to describe God? In what ways is He a fire to your heart today? Spend some time in quiet reflection on what fire is, what it does, how it changes things. Ask the Holy Spirit to illumine your heart to the reality of Jesus as *Consuming Fire* in your soul today.

READ

Read as many of the following as you can, then ponder the devotional: Isaiah 33:14; Hebrews 12:28–29; Psalm 97:3–5; Daniel 7:9; Malachi 3:2–3; 1 Corinthians 3:12–13.

For our God is a consuming fire.

HEBREWS 12:29

When the Bubonic Plague invaded the heart of London in 1665 no one was immune to its curse. Borne by fleas living as parasites on rats, the horrific disease also known as Black Death raged with ferocity, shutting down entire cities at the first sign of sickness. The streets grew empty, for as soon as one person broke out with the dreaded black lumps, the entire household was sealed, condemning them all to die. Afflicted families painted a red cross on the door, along with the words "Lord, have mercy on us." Every night workers called for the corpses, carrying them in a cart to be buried in plague pits outside the city. Truly there appeared to be no stopping the vicious killer.

If that weren't enough, a seemingly worse catastrophe struck in 1666—the Great Fire of London. With uncontainable fury a blazing inferno burst forth, engulfing building after building in flames and completely gutting much of the city's center. But in a strange twist of fate, this tragedy turned out to be a blessing in disguise, for the fire destroyed most of the black rats that had carried the plague germs. As the weeks went by following the fire's finish, the spread of the dreaded disease came to an end as well.

The irony that the Great Fire of London both destroyed *and* saved the city powerfully portrays the paradox we find in Jesus as our *Consuming Fire.* Scripture tells us that He is a continual burning, that His touch alone makes mountains smoke, that His very presence melts them. Christ's eyes are a flame of fire, His throne ablaze with flames, and He reigns from a sea of glass mixed with fire. When He returns to this earth He will be revealed amid His angels and flaming fire. The very substance of God is a fiery force that causes the earth to tremble and from whom men will one day flee in terror.[1]

And yet one dark day some two thousand years ago, the fire of God's love burned on a cross called Calvary. Bearing the sins of the world, Jesus became a holy holocaust, consuming forever the plague that had doomed humankind to hopeless devastation. Now new life springs eternally by His Spirit within those who trust in Him, and day after day He blazes through our souls, demolishing every vestige of self that threatens this life He has given.

Like the "burn" that fire fighters often purposefully set to keep future fires from blazing out of control, Christ, the *Consuming Fire,* enflames the edges of our lives, drawing ever closer to those things that seem so dear to us. In ways that can be painful and even terrifying, He makes of this world's treasures a smoldering ruin, for He knows that one day all that is not of Him will vanish like smoke before our eyes. He incinerates our worthless works in His fiery orb that our labor here might not be in vain (1 Corinthians 3:12–13).

As the *Consuming Fire,* Jesus longs for us to be sparkling gems, refined by Him to display His dazzling glory. Because He alone knows the motives and hidden secrets of our hearts, at times He intensifies the heat until it seems almost unbearable. Indeed, if not for His grace, who of us could live with His continual burning? He sits like a smelter above us, increasing the flame until the dross comes to the surface so that He can wipe it away and His glorious image may shine (Isaiah 33:14; Malachi 3:1–3).

Though our spiritual lives may seem at times like flickering wicks, there is coming a day when they will blaze brightly with the full radiance of His glory. As the writer of Hebrews assures us, we need not fear the final destruction of hell's vast flames, for we will not come to a mountain that if touched would kill us, or to a blazing fire. Instead, we will come to Mount Zion, the city of the living God, the heavenly Jerusalem. We will not come to darkness and gloom and whirlwind but to myriads of angels and to the church—people made perfect by His blood. We will not appear in fear and trembling before the terrifying voice of God but worship at the feet of Jesus, the Mediator of the new covenant.

What else can we do but let Him draw us like moths to His wondrous, penetrating flame of love and with grateful hearts serve Him in reverence and awe, for He is a *Consuming Fire* (Hebrews 12:22–29).

RESPOND

The metaphor of fire for God is a common one that teaches much about His nature. Fire destroys and preserves, protects and consumes, warms and annihilates, enlightens and blinds. In what ways have you experienced the seemingly opposite qualities of Jesus the *Consuming Fire*?

Without the protection of His blood, exposure to the blaze that is the exalted Christ would consume us. The reality of this should fill our hearts with holy fear and a depth of gratitude, resulting in reverent service. How might you increase your experience of these things in your daily walk with Christ?

Jesus comes as fire to our lives to burn up the dross, to purify our hearts, and to ensure that what we do will have lasting value. He is jealous for our worship and the works that will glorify His name. Ponder this and write a prayer of response.

A Prayer

O Consuming Fire, who beckons me, I am like a moth drawn to your holy flame. I cannot get enough, for out of the ashes of my existence, you bring new life. You blaze, and my worthless works become dust. Burn away, O loving inferno, for every death brings glorious resurrection. I live for the day I will be caught up in the combustion of your being, when your power will incinerate all that is not of you and annihilate all that does not reflect your glory. Come, Consuming Fire—enflame my heart that I might more purely worship you.

BREAD OF LIFE

Nourisher, Sustainer, Supporter, Satisfier, Provider

REFLECT

Breathe deeply as you sit before the Lord today. As you inhale, take in the wonders of His love, goodness, faithfulness, His very presence with you. As you exhale, breathe out the distractions of the day, the sins you need to confess, the busyness that draws you from His embrace.

As you take each breath, consider the truth that this very breath was granted you by Jesus, that without His permission you would cease to exist. How would your daily life change if this point were a driving, pulsing reality for you? Ask Jesus to give you a fresh awareness today of your great dependency upon and need of Him for everything. Thank Him for the blessing of life.

READ

Are there any ways in which you feel unsatisfied with your life today? Spend a few minutes jotting a list of the things in your life that do bring you joy and satisfaction. Ponder these as you read some of the following Scriptures and then the devotional: John 6:51; Psalm 23:5; Psalm 81:16; Isaiah 55:1–2; Psalm 22:26.

> *I am the bread of life;*
> *he who comes to Me will not hunger.*
>
> JOHN 6:35

Every year on the day after Thanksgiving millions of people flock to the malls, bringing consumer spending to its highest annual level and making it the best day of the year for retail manufacturers. But over the past few years a counterculture movement has sprung up calling for a moratorium on shopping that day. Purchasing ads, buying billboards, and flooding e-mail chains, the group behind "Buy Nothing Day" pleads with shoppers to take a stand by withholding their purchasing power.

Who are these people and what stand do they want us to take? They call themselves "culture jammers," a group on a mission to cure *affluenza*, a societal sickness caused by over-consumption, which they contend produces all manner of spiritual and environmental ills. Noting that America with less than 20 percent of the world's population consumes 80 percent of its resources, culture jammers spend their days finding ways to "jam" the consumer culture in which we live.

The whole idea seems a bit like David coming against Goliath—young, passionate zealots trying to take down corporate America by uprooting the greed that keeps it alive. This is no easy task in a country whose constituents last year spent $277 billion eating out, $237 billion buying clothes, and $6.6 billion going to the movies. One young man, seeking to explain the *why* of American greed, surmised: "Over-consumption is just the most obvious symptom of a larger sickness: our culture is so empty that it needs to stuff itself to feel full."[1]

In reality, over-consumption *is* a symptom of emptiness—the emptiness caused by sin in the soul of every human being. We are, by our fallen nature, so empty that no amount of glutting our stomachs or our closets or the hours in our day can fill us. Why? Because our capacity for pleasure is as infinite as the One in whose image we are made. When God created man for himself, He gave him the ability to enjoy His glory as much as He does—to see, know, revel in, and reflect the beauty of His being, that we might live to exalt Him with praise and delight (Isaiah 43:7). It was a wondrous plan, beyond human comprehension.

But sin soon entered the world, derailing this plan and destroying man's capacity for the only thing that could ever fully satisfy. Jonathan Edwards wrote that when this happened, the "excellent and enlarged condition" of man's soul was gone, "and thenceforward he himself shrank, as it were, into a little space, circumscribed and closely shut up within itself to the exclusion of all things else."[2]

To be lost in sin is to be shrunk up within oneself, ever striving to replenish a void that cannot be filled. This is the condition to which Jesus spoke when He said, *I am the bread of life; he who comes to Me will not hunger.* This unqualified utterance declares that Jesus' death on the cross bought far more than we could ever dream of, for through new birth He restores our capacity for the one thing grand enough to satisfy the human soul: the infinite glory of God.

To come to Jesus as the *Bread of Life* means we no longer need pursue the temporal treasures of this world, for in Him is immeasurable joy. To know Him is to be satiated with the riches of glory. And like the oil and flour for the Zarephath widow's bread, we find that each time we dine at the table of His delights there is a fresh feast, a repast that reaches to our depths, filling us with desire for more and more (1 Kings 17).

In claiming to be the *Bread of Life,* Jesus disclosed that we dishonor Him most by failing to find our satisfaction in Him. When we relish the passing pleasures of this world, we say by our lives that His magnificence cannot assuage the yearnings of our soul. In this we become a reproach and a grief to our Maker. Like the Israelites, we hear His voice crying out, *Why do you spend money for what is not bread, and your wages for what does not satisfy? What injustice did your fathers find in Me that they went far from Me and walked after emptiness and became empty?* (Isaiah 55:2; Jeremiah 2:5).

The only thing we must have to dine at our Lord's table is spiritual hunger, a longing in our souls for lasting joy. We come to Him empty-handed, beggars ravenous for the *Bread* that endures. And when we've tasted and seen that the Lord is good, we cannot but proclaim to an empty world that there is One who satisfies, One who quenches every desire, One who fills starving souls with His precious presence. This is the wonder of faith, the miracle of Jesus, the *Bread of Life*.

RESPOND

Every day the world holds out delightful fare, and though it may be pleasing to our palates, it will never satisfy the deepest longings of our soul. Jesus the *Bread of Life* alone has the power to satisfy us at our core. Are there longings in your soul that you fail to bring to the One who alone can satisfy the pangs of spiritual hunger? What are they?

We come to the *Bread of Life* because happiness cannot be found elsewhere. Thus our daily Christian walk should be characterized not merely by steps of obedience but as a pursuit of joy. Is this your experience? Why or why not?

When we fast from the things of this world, whether it is food, clothing, or entertainment, we are not doing without or giving something up but opening ourselves to the real *Bread of Life*. It is not a fast, but a feast—a feast on God himself, who ever lives to nourish our souls for His glory. Ponder this and write a prayer of response.

A Prayer

> O Lord, how simple you have made it—as simple as eating my necessary food. All I must do is come, believing you alone can satisfy. You are the Bread of Life, and I cannot live even one day without your nourishing my soul by your presence. Dearest One, who was broken that I might taste of glory, I am appalled that I eat the stale bread of this world, thinking I will be filled. But oh, the short-lived pleasure of dining on those hollow delights. I hunger now for manna from heaven; I pine for your presence and long for your glory to fill me once again. Come, Bread of Life, and fill me up.

DELIVERER

Emancipator, Liberator, Rescuer, Preserver

REFLECT

Read Psalm 103. For David this was a litany of all God had done for him, a desire to *forget none of His benefits.* Today write your own psalm of praise. Begin as David did: *Bless the Lord, O my soul; and all that is within me, bless His holy name. Bless the Lord, O my soul, and forget none of His benefits.* Then add a list of benefits you have received from God. Bless Him with your thankful heart. Extol His goodness. Confess ingratitude, discontent, even indifference to all He is and has done.

READ

Read at least two of the following Scriptures and the devotional: Romans 11:26–27; Colossians 1:13; Isaiah 61:1; 2 Thessalonians 1:9–10; Hebrews 2:14–15.

Just as it is written,
"The Deliverer will come from Zion."

ROMANS 11:26

Hellfire, damnation, ranting, raving, staging, and strutting—these are the memories that flood my mind of the *revivals* in my childhood church, designed I suppose to chastise the children of God and somehow scare us straight. Two weeks out of every year our entire family sat in the third pew back each night while the visiting evangelist tried to reform our ways.

I remember one preacher in particular who stormed in from the Bible belt, foaming and fuming with the gospel truth. We had to be badly backslidden, living as we did in that evil wasteland called California, and he didn't mind letting us know. By the third night, his sermons had me almost throwing up. Images of bodies writhing in flames while worms ate at their flesh overwhelmed my young imagination.

Having discovered later in life the joy of grace, I have a great distaste for the coercion of Christian behavior by the fear of hell. I always wondered why those traveling evangelists acted like we could *do* something about our depravity, like it was our responsibility to figure out a way to make ourselves better. What need had we of a *Deliverer* if we could somehow have saved ourselves? To this day I struggle with that weight, with a propensity toward works that wreaks havoc in my spiritual life.

Across the landscape of faith in America today, the pendulum has clearly swung in the other direction. Hell isn't a very popular topic. For this I tend to be grateful and relieved, yet I find myself wondering if there isn't some middle ground, some healthier place for the subject of hell than to banish it altogether.

Jesus spoke of hell often, and Scripture is replete with warnings of eternal judgment. Perhaps these words are better used not to beat backslidden believers into shape but to bolster the faithful by reminding us what our life might have been had our *Deliverer* not come. To me, the most sobering verse about hell is 2 Thessalonians 1:9: *These will pay the penalty of eternal destruction, away from the presence of the Lord and from the glory of His power.*

Whatever our images of hell might be—whether fire or worms or demonic rage—surely the most terrifying thought is that it will be a place devoid of God's presence, a condition even the most miserable creature on earth has not yet experienced. At this moment the glory of God's power holds evil at bay, preventing for a season the full effect of the Fall. It is true that all of creation groans, but it cannot compare to the hopeless groaning that will permeate an eternity of enslavement under Satan when the full force of evil explodes with no hope of it ever abating.

This is our destiny as depraved people. We have all sinned, gone our way in rebellion or apathy from the God who made us for himself. The wages of our defiance is spiritual death, a complete incapacity for God, a desperate inability to see or know or ever find Him, and endless pride that shuns His right to reign over our lives. Left to ourselves, we would face without hope an eternal prison— void in every way of the presence of God—from which we could never escape.

But ah—amazing grace, we aren't left to ourselves. The *Deliverer* has come, storming the gates of hell, breaking down the barrier of sin that forever held us in bondage. Now for us every second of life is a reminder of this glorious grace, the reality that we have been bought with a price, never to be subject to the terror of unending evil.

The *Deliverer* has come—what awe should fill our hearts. That He is coming again for us is a stunning enticement to live in joyful obedience every moment of every day. See Him even now: riding through the sky in magnificent splendor, Jesus will come to take His children home to dwell in His dazzling presence for all eternity, where we will marvel forever at the glory of His power (2 Thessalonians 1:10–11; 1 Thessalonians 4:16–17).

RESPOND

Every one of us was once a prisoner, doomed to an eternity of separation from God with absolutely no hope of escape. Today God's grace still fills this world, bringing rain on the just and the unjust. Stop for a moment and consider the presence of God being removed, the complete absence of any moral or spiritual good. What would it be like? How would it be to face that for eternity?

When God redeemed us, it was a search-and-rescue operation. Jesus our Deliverer swept into enemy territory and rescued us from the Evil One's rule. Do you see yourself as having been delivered? Of having once been completely enslaved to something you could never free yourself from? What does it mean to you that Jesus came in and rescued you, delivering you from an eternity without God? Ponder this and write a prayer of response.

A Prayer

O Mighty Deliverer, I can never forget that in my neediness and affliction, you came and rescued me. While I was a slave to sin, you died to deliver my soul. I am free, Lord, and such joy fills me as I walk in the light of your presence. Yet there is an ache within, for millions are still imprisoned and have never heard the Good News that you appointed me to bring. How do I proclaim freedom when my own liberty is shadowed by sin and obscured by the lure of this world? Once again, Lord, I feel my desperate need and I must cry out. Deliver me, O God, from the destruction of selfish desires, that I might bind up the broken-hearted in your name and set prisoners free for your glory. I am full of hope, Jesus, my Deliverer, for you have rescued me.

LOVE

Commitment, Passion, Desire, Ardor, Fervor

REFLECT

Consider the love God has bestowed upon you as you come before Him. What does it look like? How do you experience it? Jot down some thoughts concerning how you would define His love and what it has produced in your life. Thank Him and praise Him for this love that is beyond understanding.

READ

The thoughts on God's love in today's devotional may be somewhat confusing if you've not pondered them before. Spend a few minutes praying and asking God to give you true illumination as you wait upon Him. Then read a few of the following Scriptures and the devotional: Romans 8:38–39; Romans 5:8; Titus 3:4–6; 1 John 4:9–10; 1 John 4:16; Ephesians 3:16–19.

God is love.

1 JOHN 4:16

Recently I received the following in an e-mail card from a dear Christian friend:

If God had a refrigerator,
your picture would be on it.
If He had a wallet,
your photo would be in it.
What about the Christmas gift
He sent you in Bethlehem?
Not to mention that Friday at Calvary.
Face it, He's crazy about you!

Though these are warm words, to me they served as a sobering reminder that trying to write what is on my heart concerning Jesus as *Love* is going to be like swimming against the current with weights on every limb. I am well aware this message may seem in direct contradiction to decades of evangelical sentiment, and I don't take such a thing lightly.

Still I must ask, are we missing the point with sermons and songs and self-help books that seem to make Christianity all about *us*? Was it primarily His affection for *us* that brought about Jesus' birth in Bethlehem and His death on Calvary? I wrote earlier, in the introduction of my quest to discover a *different Jesus,* of my desire to extricate myself from the center of a lifetime of "Christian" thought and theology. Nowhere have I found this more difficult to do than with regard to God's love.

It began a few years ago when in a message on Christ's death, John Piper asked, "Do you love the Cross because it makes much of you, or because it enables you to make much of Jesus?"[1] I was taken aback and slightly offended, but mostly frustrated because the question didn't seem to make sense. How could the Cross *not* be about me? All my life I had heard and believed that Jesus loved *me*, suffered for *me*, bore the shame for *me*, and shed His blood for *me*. I cherished the Cross, had written a book about it, and came to it often to be bathed in the *Love* of God—what could possibly be wrong with that?

In the ensuing years God stripped me bare, first with tender assurances that He does love me with an everlasting love and that this *Love* poured out on Calvary will always be an ointment to heal my fallen soul. And yet slowly, painfully, I began to grasp the folly of turning His great love into some kind of measure of *my* value, instead of holding it forth as a banner extolling *His.* Jesus Christ is Lord; He is worthy, and He alone must be the center, the exalted One. I have grieved from the depths of my being this form of subtle idolatry, this worship of *self* that plagued my heart. I believe these roots lie hidden in the very fiber of a humanist worldview and pagan culture that inevitably translates into a man-centered Christianity.

Jesus made His purpose for living and dying abundantly clear in a prayer only hours before His arrest: *Father, the hour has come; glorify Thy Son, that the Son may glorify Thee* (John 17:1). God's supreme passion has always been that His own glory—His attributes, acts, character, and ways—might be made known throughout the earth and worshiped. When we were lost and had nothing to offer and no way to find Him, Christ suffered and bled and died in our place that we might relate to Him intimately, so that we might offer lives of worship commensurate with His worth. This is the *Love* of God manifested for sinful souls.

There is indescribable delight in recognizing that this *Love* is not really about us but about the God of the Universe, who condescends to come into our finite existence and manifest the beauty of His being. God's *Love* is exorbitant because He is eternal, merciful because He is mighty, powerful because He is preeminent, magnificent because He is majestic, and extravagant because He is extraordinary. *Love* means God will go to extreme lengths, even dying on a cross, to display His glory in and through and to us for His own exaltation and our highest joy.

This is the *Love* that both transfixes and transforms, for it knows no bounds. Indeed, an experience of this *Love* renders issues of self-esteem and personal worth irrelevant—they are simply no longer the point. He is worthy, and as our hearts truly come to know the length and height and breadth and depth of *Love,* we will delight to make much of Him, as we are filled with all the fullness of God (Ephesians 3:18).

RESPOND

Do you live with the sense that you are being filled *with all the fullness of God*? Consider John Piper's question: "Do you love the Cross because it makes much of you, or because it enables you to make much of Jesus?" How would you answer this? Why?

The love of God for sinners radiates from His passion to exalt himself for our joy. Because *agape* is best seen through Jesus' death on Calvary, we can have the assurance that God's love will go to any length to glorify himself. This is our hope. How might this kind of love encourage you in the struggles of faith you are presently experiencing? How might it motivate you to press on in obedience to the upward call of God in Christ Jesus?

This kind of love cannot be naturally understood. It requires a spiritual strength in our deepest being to grasp it at all. Spend some time asking God to reveal to your own heart the essence of *agape.* Reflect on it, and write a prayer of response.

A Prayer

O Jesus, this is a mystery beyond knowing, a wonder beyond my grasp. How can you call me to know and believe this love that is as infinite as you are? I cannot, my Lord, for its height and breadth and depth and length far exceeds the feeble confines of my mind. How I long for the day when I will shed the

AT THE NAME OF JESUS

restrictions of this frail flesh, when I can see you as you are and love you as you deserve. Until then, my Lord, come and fill me up; saturate my soul with passion for your glory; lavish upon me the desire that consumes your own heart. Let me know true agape, O Jesus, until I am lost in your splendor and live to see you glorified, being filled up at last with all of your fullness.

LORD OF GLORY

Honor, Weight, Perfection, Splendor,
Brightness, Emanation, Manifestation

REFLECT

Let today be a time of great exulting in the presence of Jesus. Think of all you have seen of Him and of all you have yet to see. Read Psalm 24:7–10 as a proclamation, inviting the very presence of your glorious Savior, Jesus Christ, to manifest himself in you and through you this day. Welcome Him, enjoy Him, delight in His ways, and live for His purposes. Ponder His perfection. Wait upon Him, asking Him once again to give you a spirit of wisdom and revelation in the knowledge of Him.

READ

Read these Scriptures and the following devotional: Hebrews 1:3; 2 Thessalonians 2:14; 1 Corinthians 2:7–8; 2 Corinthians 3:18.

For if they had understood it they would not have crucified the Lord of glory.

1 CORINTHIANS 2:8

The science section located in our daily newspaper on Wednesdays has been for me a source of pleasure since it first started detailing discoveries of the cosmos made possible by the launching of NASA's Hubble Space Telescope. Sort of a robotic camera in the sky, the Hubble orbits Earth once every ninety-seven minutes at an altitude of about three hundred and seventy miles, snapping picture after glorious picture. Where astronomers were once limited to what they could observe beneath Earth's atmosphere, the space telescope has opened up a detailed view of "the fascinating complexity and diversity of the universe, as well as its startling beauty."[1]

Even the most seasoned astronomers have been taken aback at what they've seen. For example, they've discovered that billions of stars radiate in the heavens in hues of red, yellow, white, blue, and orange, and that in dying, these do not fade out but instead dramatically blow off their outer layers. When this happens, stars disintegrate into spectacular celestial fireworks sort of like a wild all-night disco party, leaving in their wake objects of great structural detail—bizarre shapes like Cat's Eye Nebula, whose gases resemble a twirling lawn sprinkler.[2]

Stephen Charnock, a seventeenth-century theologian, wrote that in the heavens God's "majesty is most visible," suggesting that while we on earth only enjoy the beams of God's splendid glory, its fullness is found in the firmament.[3] The Hubble Space Telescope may verify his theory, and it surely confirms the psalmist's cry that the heavens declare the glory of God, day to day pouring forth speech, night after night revealing knowledge (Psalm 19:1–2).

While the living God has always delighted in these mysteries humankind is only beginning to uncover, there is a greater glory, a more profound sight that burns in His heart with rapturous joy. It is Jesus, His Son, the *Lord of Glory,* who perfectly reflects the panorama of God's own perfections[4]—His grandeur, majesty, mystery, and matchless magnificence—in a spectacle of splendor such that no night sky could ever compare.

The word *glory* in Scripture reverberates with wonder. The glory of God refers to His self-revelation, the manifestation of His essence without which we would have no grasp of Him at all. The Hebrew Scriptures spoke of God's glory as His *kabhodh,* meaning *weight* or *heaviness,* indicating that the very presence of God is so awesome that it carries with it a weight, at times palpable. One of the Greek words for *glory* was *doxa,* which commonly spoke of brightness, brilliance, or splendor.[5]

Thus when Scripture refers to Jesus as *Lord of Glory,* it affirms that no person or any thing can more supremely manifest the resplendent brilliance of all that God is than Christ, for He is the very radiance of the Father. The significance of this is unfathomable because we see through a glass darkly and cannot yet comprehend what the fullness of glory resting in the bosom of our Lord portends.

The glory of God encompasses all that He is—every attribute and characteristic we might conceive and thousands more. When the Father looks to the Son, He sees the sum total of His dazzling deity, and delight springs from His depths. *This is my beloved Son, with whom I am well pleased,* His voice boomed on the Mount of Transfiguration, and the terrified disciples fell, faces to the ground. For us to gaze at Jesus, *Lord of Glory,* is to be enthralled with the wonder of Him, ever exulting in hope of the day when at last we will be set free from the shackles of flesh that obscure our view.

Jesus, *Lord of Glory*—let us meditate on His majesty, ponder His power, delight in His dominion, savor His sufficiency, tremble at His truth, contemplate His compassion, wrestle with His wrath, praise His patience, glean from His goodness, grapple with His grace, muse on His mercy, and hide in His holiness. This is our call, our cause, the pulsating purpose of life both now and into eternity—that we might gain the glory of our Lord Jesus Christ (2 Thessalonians 2:14). Hallelujah! Sound forth His praises, sing of His worth: Jesus, *Lord of Glory*.

RESPOND

The glory of God is a concept so massive it is impossible to articulate. It refers to all that He is and does and then to our response of worship for what we have seen of Him. God exhibits His glory, we experience Him, and then exult in joy-filled worship. God reveals His glory, we revere, and then revel in the delight of following Him. God shows His glory, we savor it, then shine forth in His very image. In what ways have you begun to see this worked out in your own life?

Jesus, Son of God, is the Lord of Glory, radiant in the very beauty of divine essence. He is supreme and perfect in every facet of His Being. To know Him is to be in awe of Him, to fall at His feet in wonder and worship. As you consider the days you have spent meditating on Jesus, how has your view of Him expanded? In what ways do you see yourself offering worship worthy of His greatness?

To gain the glory of Jesus Christ is to live with the experience of Him, not merely knowledge about Him, but to see with spiritual eyes and be moved at the very depths of who we are by what we have seen. This, Paul says, is the purpose to which we have been called. What does this mean to you? Write a prayer of response.

A Prayer

Unbounding Lord of Glory, you have tantalized me with a taste, and I am famished for want of more of you. I yearn for you in your essence, crying out as Moses did, "Lord, show me your glory." Should you manifest the weight of your very Being, the blind would see, the lame walk, the broken be restored, and the evil one flee. If you came, O Lord of glory, cold hearts would be enflamed, dead spirits brought to life, and our lives revolutionized by everlasting joy. This cry you've put within me is becoming a desperate plea: night and day I long for you to fill the earth with your glory as the waters cover the sea. My destiny and my driving passion is that you might manifest your glory, today and every day. I exult in the hope of glory and live for that moment when time will at last stand still and you come once again, awesome, precious Jesus, Lord of Glory.

ENDNOTES

Day One

1. Prayer based on 1 John 5:20.

Day Two

1. Shawn Madigan, ed., *A Historical Anthology of Women's Spiritual Writings* (Minneapolis: Fortress Press, 1998), 24.

Day Three

1. Annie Dillard, *An American Childhood* (New York: Harper & Row, 1987), 135.
2. I believe we receive the Holy Spirit when we come to Christ in the same *positional* way we receive the mind of Christ and the power that raised Him from the dead. The problem, it seems to me, comes when we assume that we are experiencing on a practical level that which can never be fully experienced in this life or the next. If God is infinite, how can we ever fully experience Him or know His mind or demonstrate His power?

Day Four

1. Ronald Kotuiak, "Part and Particle," *San Diego Union Tribune*, January 10, 2001.

Day Five

1. W. Graham Scroggie, *The Unfolding Drama of Redemption* (Grand Rapids: Kregel Publications, 1994), 31.
2. For this graphic picture of man-centeredness, I thank missiologist George Verwer.

Day Six

1. *One of Us,* lyrics and music by Eric Bazilian, copyright © 1995, PolyGram Records, Inc. ASCAP/BMI.
2. Daniel Fuller, *The Unity of the Bible* (Grand Rapids: Zondervan Publishing House, 1992), 210.

Day Seven

1. Exodus 24; Isaiah 6; Ezekiel 1; Daniel 7; 1 Corinthians 12.
2. The well-known motto of the Moravian missionary movement.
3. Hyman Appelman, *When the Spirit Came* (Minneapolis: Bethany House Publishers, 1967), 15–16.
4. John Piper, *Let the Nations Be Glad* (Grand Rapids: Baker Books, 1993), 15.
5. In the Old Testament the Hebrew word *Goy* is translated *people(s)* and *nations,* referring to a group of individuals who are considered as a unit with respect to origin, language, land, jurisprudence, and government. The New Testament word *ethnos* is translated *nations* and *Gentiles,* referring to a race, and specifically a tribe within a race (*Vine's Expository Dictionary of Biblical Words,* [Nashville: Thomas Nelson Publishers, 1985]).

Day Eight

1. Mike Bickle, Kansas City International House of Prayer.

Day Nine

1. Wesley L. Duewel, *Mighty Prevailing Prayer* (Grand Rapids: Zondervan, 1990), 236.

Day Ten

1. I've taken a little liberty with the dialogue here. See Exodus 3:13.
2. I am indebted to Daniel Fuller's *Unity of the Bible* for its clarification

that the mandates of Scripture are not a job description for laborers but a doctor's prescription for patients.

3. A. W. Tozer, *The Divine Conquest* (Camp Hill, Pennsylvania: Christian Publications, 1950), 21.

Day Eleven

1. David Wells, *God in the Wasteland* (Grand Rapids: Eerdmans, 1994), 101.
2. David Hazard, ed., *Early Will I Seek You: A 40-Day Journey in the Company of Augustine* (Minneapolis: Bethany House, 1991), 24.
3. Steve Hawthorne, *Seek God for the City 2001* (Arlington, Texas: Waymakers, 2001), 25.

Day Twelve

1. A group of scholars gathered by the Westar Institute in 1985 to renew the quest for the historical Jesus and report its results.
2. For these and dozens more, peruse the book of Matthew, especially the Sermon on the Mount.

Day Thirteen

1. Strong's definition: *elpis* (el-pece'); from a primary *elpo* (to anticipate, usually with pleasure); expectation (abstractly or concretely) or confidence.
2. From message given at memorial service, text on: *www.abwe.org/family/memorials/service_michigan.htm*

Day Fourteen

1. William Ernest Hensley, "Invictus," 1885, public domain.
2. Charles Spurgeon, *Spurgeon's Encyclopedia of Sermons,* electronic database, copyright © 1996 by Biblesoft.

Day Fifteen

1. See *Contemplating the Cross: A Pilgrimage of Prayer* (Minneapolis: Bethany House Publishers, 1998).
2. Ibid., 175.

Day Sixteen

1. John Piper, *A Hunger for God* (Wheaton: Crossway Publishing, 1997).

Day Seventeen

1. Greek word for *ultimate power*, from which we derive our word *dynamite*.

Day Twenty

1. George Barna, *The Second Coming of the Church* (Nashville: Word Publishing, 1998).

Day Twenty-Two

1. Leo Tolstoy, *Confession*, public domain, published on the Internet by various sources, also in print by Penguin and W. W. Norton publishers.

Day Twenty-Three

1. *The Confession of St. Patrick*, translated from the Latin by Ludwig Bieler, public domain.

Day Twenty-Four

1. *Strong's Greek/Hebrew Dictionary*, electronic database, copyright © 1996 by Biblesoft.

Day Twenty-Five

1. J. J. Kritzinger, (Dons), "The Rwandan Tragedy As Public Indictment Against Christian Mission"; missiological reflections of an observer, *Missionalia*, the journal of the Southern African Missiological Society, article reprinted at *http://www.geocities.com/Athens/Parthenon/8409/rwanda1.htm*.
2. Anonymous, "To Rwanda With Love: A Report on a Delegation of Canadian Church Leaders to Rwanda During March 2001." A ministry of Upstream: *http://www.upstream.ca/Rwanda*.
3. John Calvin, as quoted in *Barnes Notes*, electronic database, copyright © 1996 by Biblesoft.

Day Twenty-Seven

1. Isaiah 33:14; Micah 1:4; Daniel 7:9; Revelation 1:14; 15:2; Isaiah 2:19; 13:13.

Day Twenty-Eight

1. See their Web site, *Adbusters.org*, for a fuller explanation and philosophy of this movement.
2. Jonathan Edwards, *The Spirit of Charity: The Opposite of a Selfish Spirit,* public domain, published online at *www.Jonathanedwards.com.*

Day Thirty

1. For more information on the ministry of John Piper, see *Desiring-God.org* on the World Wide Web.

Day Thirty-One

1. Mark Voit, *Hubble Space Telescope: New Views of the Universe* (New York: Harry N. Abrams, 2000), 3.
2. Bruce Balick, "Death in Deep Space," *San Diego Union Tribune,* November 10, 1999.
3. Stephen Charnock, *The Existence and Attributes of God* (Grand Rapids: Baker Books, 1996), 361.
4. John Piper, *The Pleasures of God* (Sisters, Oregon: Multnomah, 2000), 43.
5. *International Standard Bible Encyclopaedia,* electronic database, copyright © 1996 by Biblesoft.